SPELLING MATTERS

BOOK 1

Andrew J Woods

LONGMAN

Addison Wesley Longman Australia Pty Limited
95 Coventry Street
South Melbourne 3205 Australia

Offices in Sydney, Brisbane and Perth,
and associated companies throughout the world.

First published 1993
Reprinted 1994, 1995 (twice), 1996, 1997 (twice), 1998 (twice), 2000

Edited by Robin Bower
Designed by Mary Kerr
Illustrated by Peter Paul Bajer
Set in Helvetica 14/30
Produced by Addison Wesley Longman Australia Pty Ltd
Printed in Malaysia, PP

ISBN 0 582 80141 9

The publisher's policy is to use **paper manufactured from sustainable forests**

Contents

To the Teacher and Parent

Welcome to Spelling Matters Book 1. The Spelling Matters series has been developed to allow both the classroom teacher and the parent to improve children's word attack skills and vocabulary range.

This book contains 40 work units (36 Classroom Exercises and Fast Finishers and 4 Classroom Reviews).

Classroom Exercise

At the beginning of each exercise is a list of words. The words in this list will have some relationship with one another. The Classroom Exercise provides a variety of activities related, not only to the structure of the list words, but also to their meanings and usage.

For Fast Finishers

As the name implies, this page is provided as an extension exercise. It is recommended that this page be perhaps started in the classroom and finished at home, thereby providing parents with the opportunity to become involved in the child's learning process.

Rhymes, which incorporate relevant List words, are provided at the beginning of each Fast Finishers page. These rhymes should be drawn to the attention of students to demonstrate how words in the List can be used in our language.

Testing

If teachers choose to test students at this level, it is suggested that testing be in the form of dictation sentences which place the words into a language context.

A Record of Progress is provided on page 89 for teachers, parents and/or students to record spelling competence.

Spelling Reference List

At the back of the book is an alphabetical list of all the List words used throughout the Classroom Exercises. This list can also be used as a checklist which will note strengths and weaknesses in individual students.

Also provided is a space for students to add their own words used in their own writing.

Supplementary Activities

Teachers may find some of the following suggested activities useful in supplementing the students' work from this book.

To the Teacher and Parent

Expanding on List words

When students are working on a particular unit, have them construct lists of other words with the same characteristic(s) as the List words. Display these lists so that children can consult them during writing sessions.

Collections

Have children make collections of words with unusual or interesting characteristics. For example:

a Palindromes—dad mum level noon

b Words which spell a different word when written backwards:
dog—god net—ten
stop—pots pans—snap

c Words without vowels—why fly cry

d Words with a certain number of vowels:
4 vowels—kangaroo satellite
3 vowels—yesterday playtime
2 vowels—bee book

e Words containing smaller words:
sway—way shut—hut mother—moth

Alphabetical order

As a class exercise, write the List words in alphabetical order and display them in this order (an important prerequisite for dictionary use).

Ask which word would come first in a dictionary? Why?

Which List words would come between ___ and ___ in a dictionary?

Acrostics

Form funny, silly, or sensible sentences using letters of List words as the initial letters of each word in the sentence. For example:

Dad—Do alligators dance?

Illustrate the sentence.

Synonyms and antonyms

Make a class thesaurus using the List words. Include an antonym section.
For example:

Stop: halt end finish cease
ANT: go start begin

To the Teacher and Parent

Homographs

Identify words which:

a sound the same but are spelt differently, for example, been bean.

b sound differently but are spelt the same, for example, bow bow.

Story writing—write wall stories

How many of the List words can we include in our story?

Make lists of compound words from List words.

For example:

gum—gumboots gum tree bubblegum
camp—campfire campsite
ship—shipshape battleship shipyard

Build up word families

For example:

shop—shops shopper shopping shopped
win—winner wins won winning

Use List words to develop further interest lists

For example:

dog

puppy	bark	Border Collie
Pal	wag	Boxer
	woof	Jack Russell

Rhyming couplets

Provide students with simple rhyming couplets with one of the rhyming words missing.

For example:

There was a robot named Nin
Whose undies were made out of ___

Try rhyming quatrains.

To the Student

How to Be a Better Speller

Look at the word

Can you group any of the letters?

Cover the word

Think of the word/of the letter groups

Write the word

Check you are correct

If you made a mistake—Don't Panic—try again.

> Ask yourself—why did I make a mistake?
>
> If you can answer the question, you won't make the mistake again.
>
> If you can't answer the question, try using a trick.
>
> For example: **clock**   See the lock (C the L O C K) = CLOCK

Classroom Unit 1 The Alphabet

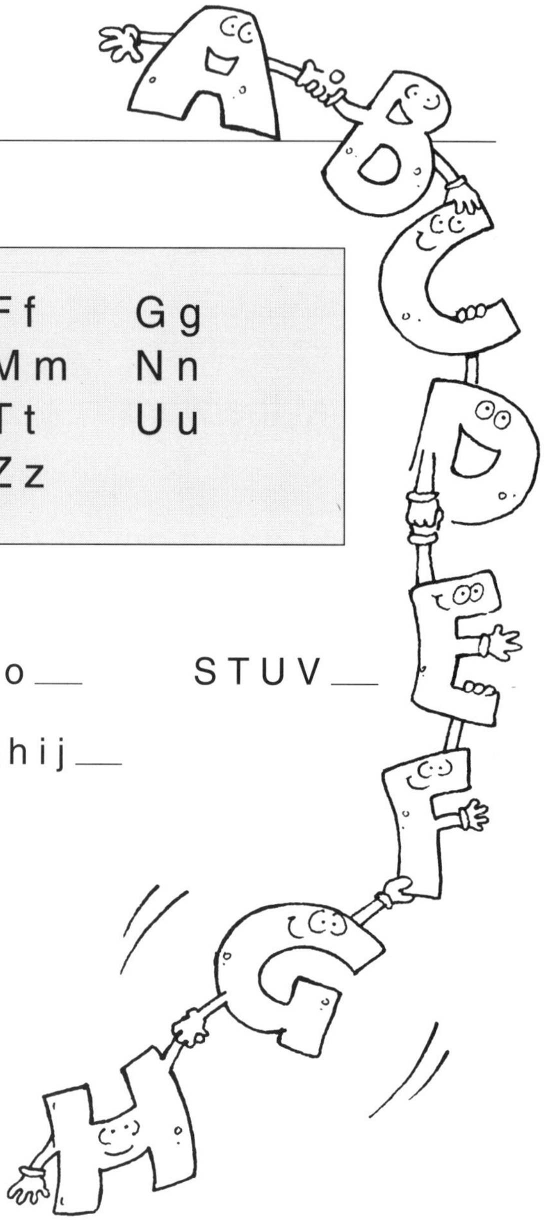

Here is the alphabet…

A a	B b	C c	D d	E e	F f	G g
H h	I i	J j	K k	L l	M m	N n
O o	P p	Q q	R r	S s	T t	U u
	V v	W w	X x	Y y	Z z	

1 What comes next?

A B C D ___ v w x y z ___ j k l m n o ___ S T U V ___

E F G H ___ o p q r ___ c d e f g h i j ___

2 What comes after?

p ___ C ___ f ___ W ___

3 What comes before?

N ___ t ___ d ___ S ___

4 Copy…

A ___ E ___ I ___ O ___ U ___

a ___ e ___ i ___ o ___ u ___

5 Finish these alphabet clocks…

For Fast Finishers

1 Which letter do I begin with?

A was an apple pie

A was an apple pie,
B bit it,
C cut it,
D dealt it,
E eat it,
F fought for it,
G got it,
H had it,
I inspected it,
J jumped for it,
K kept it,
L longed for it,
M mourned for it,
N nodded at it,
O opened it,
P peeped in it,
Q quartered it
R ran for it,
S stole it,
T took it,
U upset it,
V viewed it,
W wanted it,
X, Y, Z and ampersand (&)
All wished for a piece in hand.

2 Draw… something beginning with…

B b **M m** **T t**

Classroom Unit 2 b as in bag

Your List

bat	bad	bag	bed	bin
big	box	bun	bus	but

1 Write the missing letter…

___ i g ___ i n ___ u s ___ u n

2 Match…

bat

bag

bus

bun

3 Copy…

box ___ ___ ___ but ___ ___ ___ bin ___ ___ ___

bad ___ ___ ___ bag ___ ___ ___ bed ___ ___ ___

4 I am written backwards—write me correctly…

d e b ____________ s u b ____________ t u b ____________

5 What am I ?

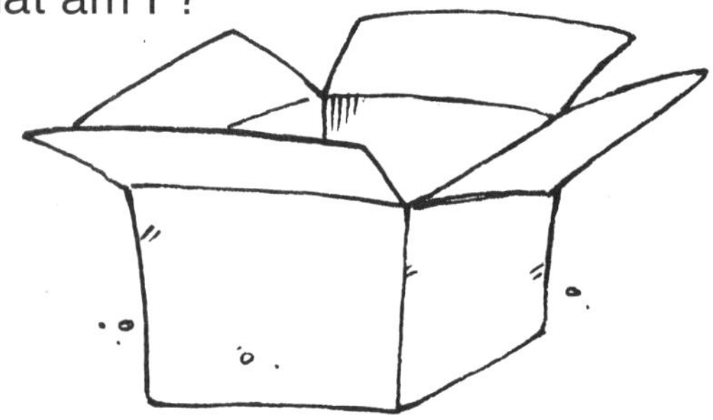

___ ___ ___ ___ ___ ___

For Fast Finishers

Benny bit a burger bun,
The burger bun bit Benny.
Benny bit it back again—
It only cost a penny.

1 Draw…

a fat bat

a rag bag

a red bed

2 Finish this Wordcross…

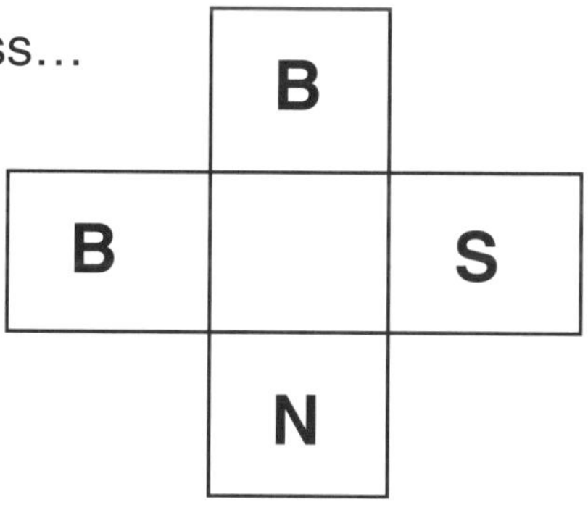

Down: you can eat me

Across: you can ride in me

3 Write the **list** words that you can see in this picture…

__________ __________ __________

__________ __________

4 Which **list** words fit into this Wordframe?

__________ __________

__________ __________

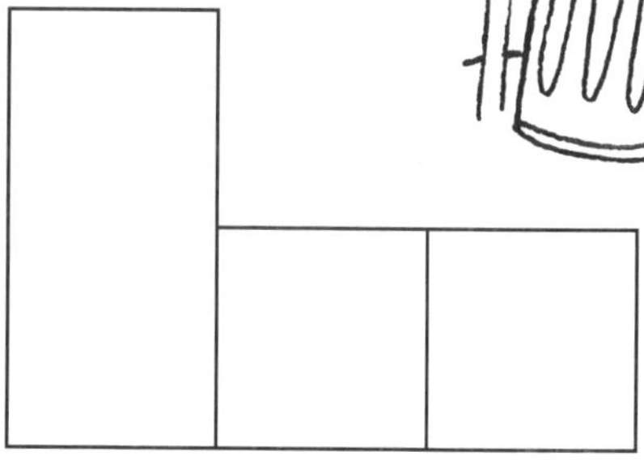

Classroom Unit 3 d as in dog

Your List

dad	dig	dog	dam	den
did	dim	dip	dot	do

1 Tick when you can say…

did ◯ dim ◯ dig ◯ dip ◯

dad ◯ dam ◯

dog ◯ dot ◯

den ◯

do ◯

2 Write the missing letters…

__ o g __ o t __ a m __ e n

3 Yes or No?

Do dogs run? ____________

Do dots dig dams? ____________

Do foxes dig dens? ____________

4 Write **list** words in the gaps…

The  ____________ lives in a  ____________

near the  ____________.

5 I am written backwards—write me correctly…

m a d ____________ d i d ____________ d a d ____________

t o d ____________ n e d ____________ p i d ____________

For Fast Finishers

I'll teach my dog 100
words.
The first six words
I'll teach my pup
are...
dig a hole !
and...
fill it up !
(Michael Frith)

1 Which **list** words... ?

__________ __________ __________

2 Which **list** word is hidden here ?

a	d	d	a	d	b	a	b	d	a

____

3 Word sums...

d + ot = __________ di + m = __________ d + o = __________

d + i + d = __________ d + e + n = __________ d + ig = __________

4 Circle the words that match the pictures...

dam
dim
den

did
dad
dig

5 Think! Which six words did Michael teach his dog first ?

__________ __________ __________ __________

__________ __________

Classroom Unit 4 t as in tap

Your List

tap	ten	tin	top	tip
tag	tan	tub	tug	to

1 I am written backwards—write me correctly…

b u t ____________ p o t ____________ n e t ____________

p a t ____________ n i t ____________ p i t ____________

2 Write the missing letters…

__ u g __ a g __ a n __ o

__ o p __ u b __ e n __ i p

3 Which word ?

____

____

____

____

4 Yes or No?

Can a tap drip ? ____________

Can you tug a tag ? ____________

Can a tin get a tan ? ____________

5 Which word does not belong… ?

tip top but tub tap ____________

For Fast Finishers

Tip-top tip-top
tap a speckled egg.
Once to put him in his cup
and twice to crack his head.
(Michael Rosen)

1 Which letter is missing from this Wordcross ?

	T	
T		B
	G	

2 Write the third (3rd) letter of each word…

ten ___ tip ___ tag ___ tub ___

3 Tick when you can say…

tap ◯ tag ◯ tan ◯

tug ◯ tub ◯

tip ◯ tin ◯

ten ◯

top ◯

to ◯

4 Draw…

ten tins

a tug in a tub

5 Think !

I am a **list** word. I am the very end of something. ______________

I am a **list** word. I mean to pull. ______________

Classroom Unit 5 g as in gum

Your List

get	gun	got	god
gas	gap	gum	go

1 Copy…

gun ___ ___ ___ gap ___ ___ ___

gas ___ ___ ___ gum ___ ___ ___ get ___ ___ ___

got ___ ___ ___ god ___ ___ ___ go ___ ___

2 Which **list** words… ?

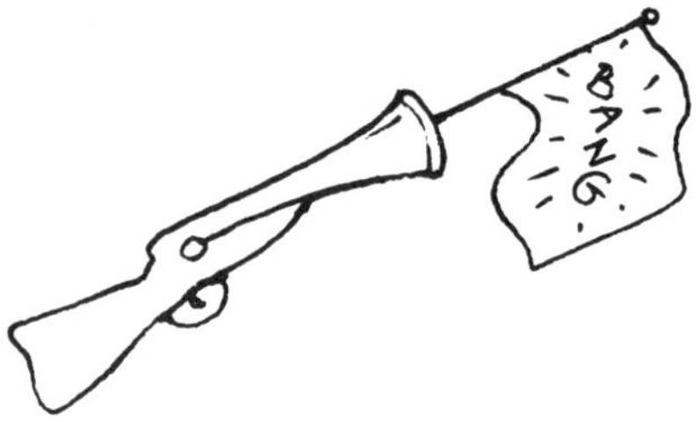

____

____

3 Which **list** words can you make ?

as ot __________ __________

g +

od um __________ __________

4 Draw… a gum tree

5 Write the missing letters…

___ e t ___ o t ___ o d

___ o ___ a p ___ u n

For Fast Finishers

1 Which **list** words… ?

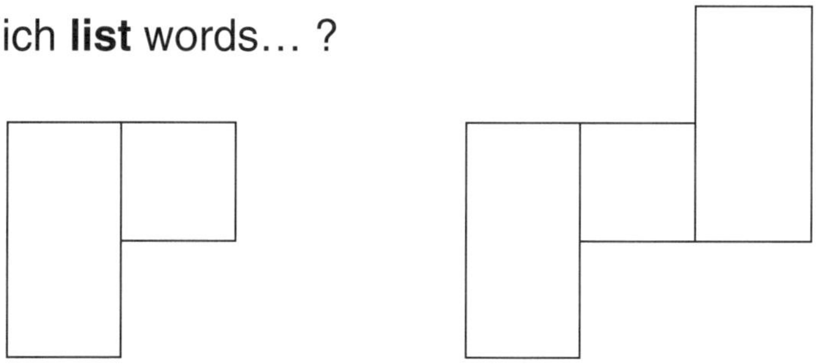

2 Think! Write a **list** word in the gap…

Chew and blow your bubble ______________ .

3 Which two **list** words are hidden in

this Wordfind ?

g	u	g	u	n	n	o	t	g	o	t	g

____

____

4 Word sums…

g + et = ______________ g + a + s = ______________

go + d = ______________ g + a + p = ______________

5 Write a sentence using these words…

gun ______________________________________

got ______________________________________

Bubble gum, bubble gum,
Chew and blow,
Bubble gum, bubble gum,
Scrape your toe,
Bubble gum, bubble gum,
Tastes so sweet,
Get that bubble gum
Off your feet.

Classroom Unit 6 p as in pet

Your List

pan	pin	pet	pat	peg
pig	pop	pup	pip	pit

1 Which **list** words… ?

g i p ______ o p p ______ t e p ______

n p a ______ p p i ______ t i p ______

2 Circle the words that match the pictures…

pop
pip
pup

pig
pan
peg

pin
peg
pit

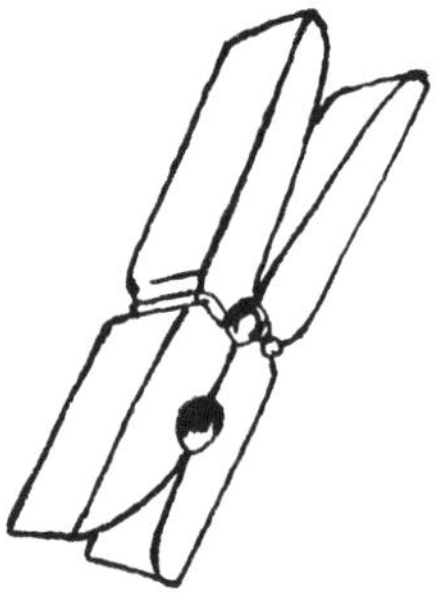

3 Write a sentence with…

pet ______

pat ______

4 Which word fits best… ?

You can cook in me ______ I snort ______

You can pat me ______ I hold washing ______

5 Copy…

pop ______ pip ______ peg ______ pup ______

pit ______ pig ______ pin ______ pet ______

For Fast Finishers

Pit - a - pat
What was that?
Six fat raindrops
On my hat.

1 Think! How many raindrops on my hat? ______________

2 Which **list** words can you find in these Wordclocks?

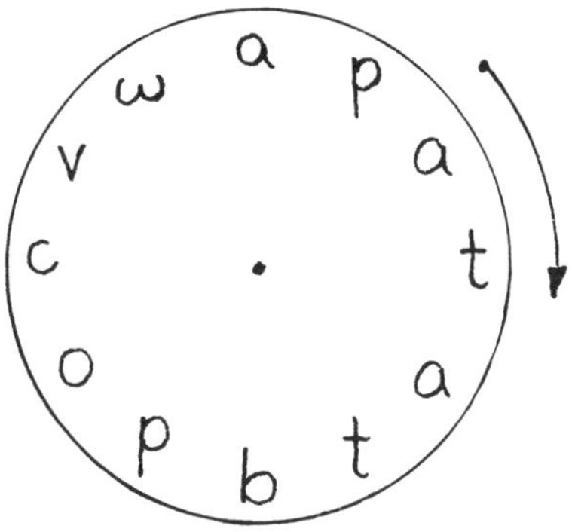

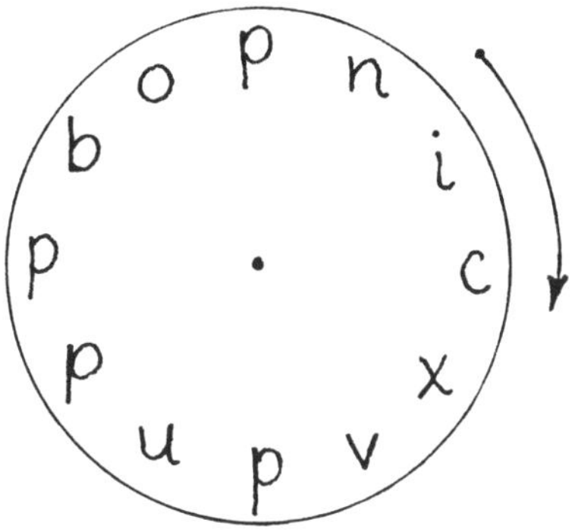

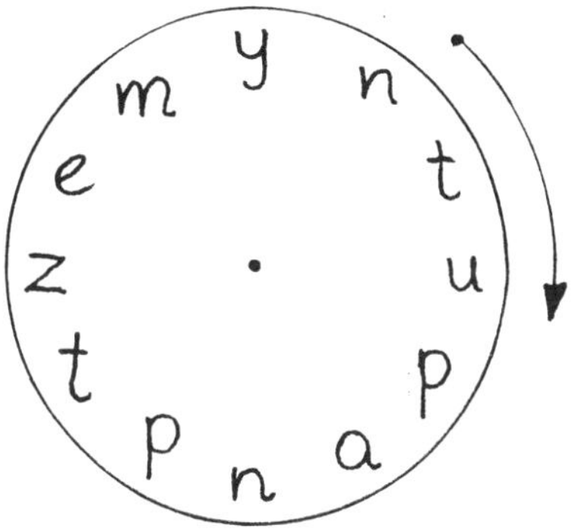

______________ ______________ ______________

3 Which **list** words would fit into this Wordframe?

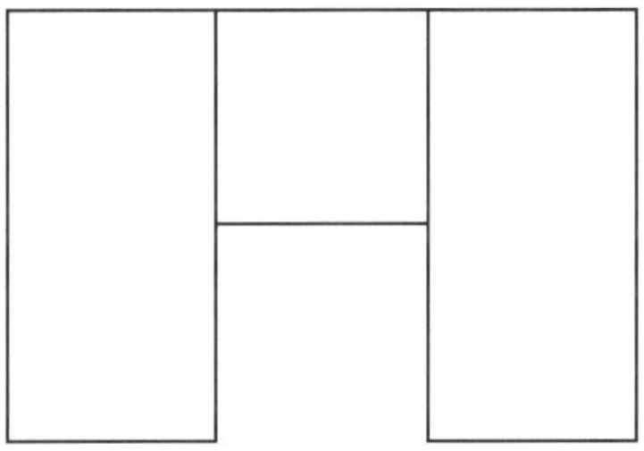

______________ ______________ ______________

______________ ______________

4 What am I? I hold things together ______________

I am a fruit seed ______________

5 Do you have a pet? Draw it here…

If you don't have a pet draw…

…a pig in a pan.

Classroom Unit 7 a as in bat and can

Your List

bat	hat	sat	cat	mat
can	pan	tap	dad	bad

1 Copy… bat ____________ hat ____________ mat ____________

cat ____________ dad ____________ pan ____________ tap ____________

bad ____________ can ____________ sat ____________

2 Draw…

a can and a pan

tap-dancing dad

3 Yes or No? You can hit with a bat ____________

You can sit on a bad ____________

4 Name…

__ a t

__ a t

__ ap

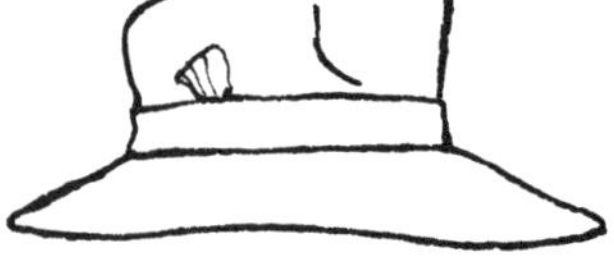

__ at

For Fast Finishers

Dame Trot and her cat
Sat down for a chat;
The Dame sat on her side
And puss sat on that.

1 Which words… ?

	a	t
	a	t
	a	t
	a	t

2 Which **list** words are hidden in these Wordfinds?

x	u	p	a	n	v	t	a	s	o

____

a	n	p	c	o	t	v	t	a	p

____

3 Word sums…

d + ad = ______________ sa + t = ______________ b + a + d = ______________

4 What is happening?

Tell someone or write what you think is happening in this picture…

____

____

____

____

____

Classroom Unit 8 e as in bed and pen

Your List

bed	pen	red	yes	get
hen	ten	men	pet	wet

1 Copy…

bed ______ red ______ hen ______

ten ______ men ______ pen ______ get ______

yes ______ pet ______ wet ______

2 Which words… ?

___ ___ ___

___ ___ ___

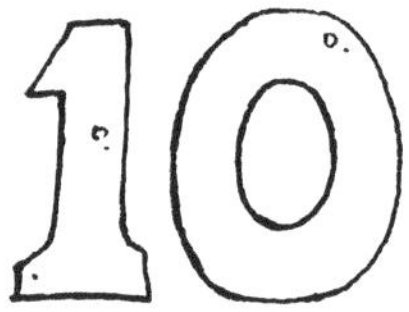

___ ___ ___

3 Draw… a pet in a red pen

4 Tick when you can say…

bed ◯ red ◯

get ◯ wet ◯ pet ◯

yes ◯

hen ◯ ten ◯ men ◯ pen ◯

5 Yes or No?

Is the sky red ? ______

Can a hen cluck ? ______

Can men write with pens ? ______

Can a pet get wet ? ______

Do hens sleep in wet beds ? ______

For Fast Finishers

Higgledy — Piggledy
My black hen,
She lays eggs for gentlemen;
Sometimes nine,
And sometimes ten,
Higgledy — Piggledy
My black hen!

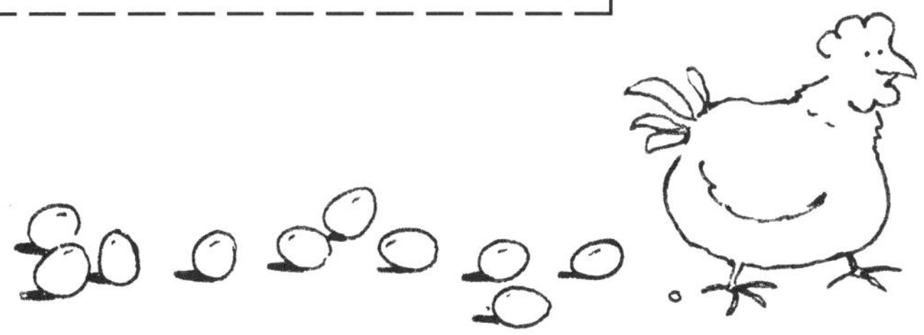

1 Think! How many eggs

can my black hen lay? ______________

2 Where is the pet? Tick.

◯ on a hen

◯ under a bed

◯ in a pen

3 Which words… ?

	e	n
	e	t
	e	n
	e	n
	e	t

4 Crossword…

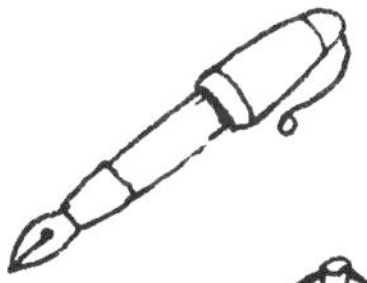

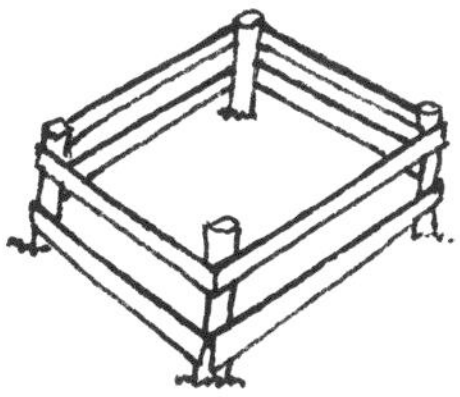

p		t
n		n

5 Colour the **list** words in this picture red.

Classroom Unit 9 i as in pin and lid

Your List

pin	bin	lid	did	hit
tin	pig	six	dig	in

1 Tick when you can say…

lid did hit tin

six dig in bin

pin pig

2 Copy…

pin ____________ pig ____________ bin ____________ six ____________

hit ____________ did ____________ tin ____________ dig ____________

in ____________ lid ____________

3 Draw… a pig in a bin with a tin lid on its head.

4 Circle the correct word…

bin
six
dig

pig
lid
pin

tin
hit
six

For Fast Finishers

To market, to market, to buy a fat pig
Home again, home again, jiggety – jig.

1 Think! Why did we go to market? ______________________

2 We are written backwards—write us correctly…

t i h ____________ d i l ____________ n i b ____________

x i s ____________ g i d ____________ n i p ____________

3 Which **list** word is hidden in this Wordfind… ?

p	n	i	s	i	x	t	i	l	d	g	i

____

4 Write **list** words in the gaps in these sentences…

The milk came out in a ____________.

The pig hid in the ____________.

5 Which **list** words can you see in this picture ? Write them on the lines.

____

____

____

____

____

Classroom Unit 10 o as in pot and box

Your List

pot	box	dog	not	off
stop	hot	top	log	on

1 Which **list** words… ?

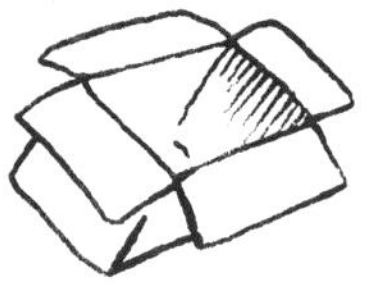
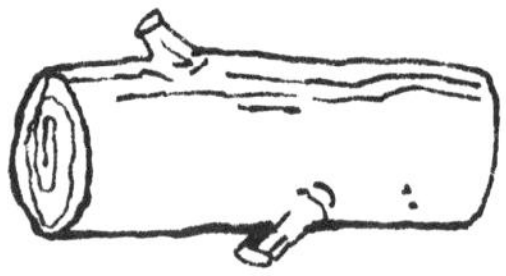
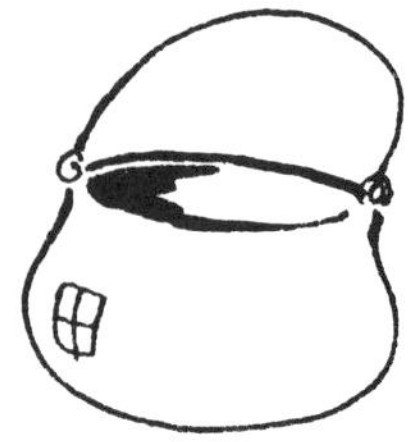

________________ ________________ ________________

2 Write the missing letters…

p __ t   d __ g   s t __ p   l __ g

t o __   b o __   n __ t   __ o t

3 Copy…

not ____________ off ____________ stop ____________ hot ____________

on ____________ log ____________ box ____________ dog ____________

pot ____________ top ____________

4 Tick when you can say…

pot ◯ box ◯ dog ◯ stop ◯

off ◯ top ◯ hot ◯ not ◯

on ◯ log ◯

5 Yes or No?

Can a box have a top? ________________

Can a log sit on a dog? ________________

Can a pot be hot? ________________

For Fast Finishers

Davy Davy Dumpling,
Boil him in a pot;
Sugar him and butter him;
And eat him while he's hot.

1 Think! When should you eat Davy? While he's ______________.

Where do you boil Davy? In a ______________.

2 Which letter is missing from this Wordcross?

	h	
n		**t**
	t	

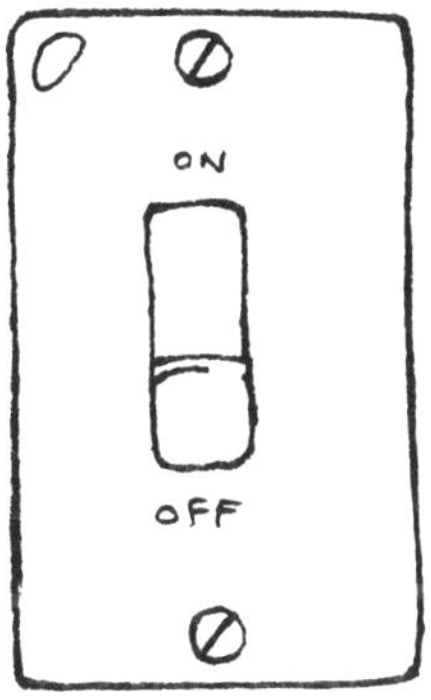

3 Label this light switch on and off…

____

____

4 Draw…

a hot pot

a top dog

5 Finish these Word sums… st + o + p = ______________

p + o + t = ______________ o + ff = ______________ o + n = ______________

Classroom Unit 11 u as in bun and pup

Your List

bun	pup	bus	run	up
cup	fun	but	sun	hut

1 Copy… bun ____________ pup ____________ bus ____________

run ____________ up ____________ cup ____________ fun ____________

but ____________ sun ____________ hut ____________

2 Fill in the missing letters…

__ u n 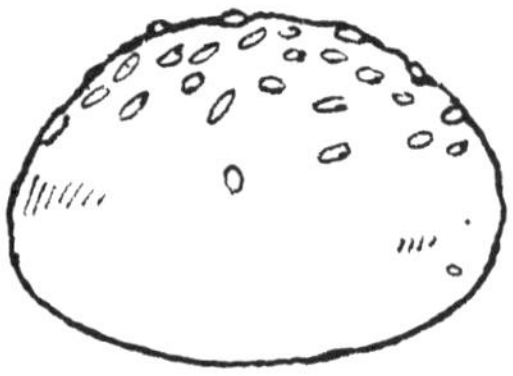

__ u s 

__ u p 

__ u t 

3 Draw… a pup having fun in the sun.

4 Write the word but in the gaps…

I am tall ____________ Tom is small.

A pup can run ____________ a hut cannot.

The sun is hot ____________ snow is not.

5 Yes or No?

Can a pup run ? ____________ Can you fill a cup ? ____________

Is the sun hut ? ____________ Can you eat a bus ? ____________

For Fast Finishers

Hot cross buns!

Hot cross buns!

One a penny, two a penny,

Hot cross buns!

1 Which words…? fun or fan ______________

sun or son

____

pup or pop

____

2 We are written backwards—write us correctly…

t u h ______________ n u b ______________ t u b ______________

3 Which **list** words are hidden in this Wordfind ?

a	f	u	n	o	p	u	p	b	u	s	o	x	c	u	p	y	b	u	t

______________ ______________ ______________ ______________ ______________

4 Colour the pictures which are **list** words…

5 Write the **list** words that you can see in this picture…

____

____

____

____

Classroom Review 1

Your List				
bet	dug	top	gap	pat
ran	off	pit	stop	rim

1 Copy…

bet ________ dug ________ top ________

gap ________ pat ________ ran ________ off ________

pit ________ stop ________ rim ________

2 Which **list** words rhyme with these…?

rug hug bug ________ map lap tap ________

him dim swim ________ fit sit bit ________

let get met ________ man tan ban ________

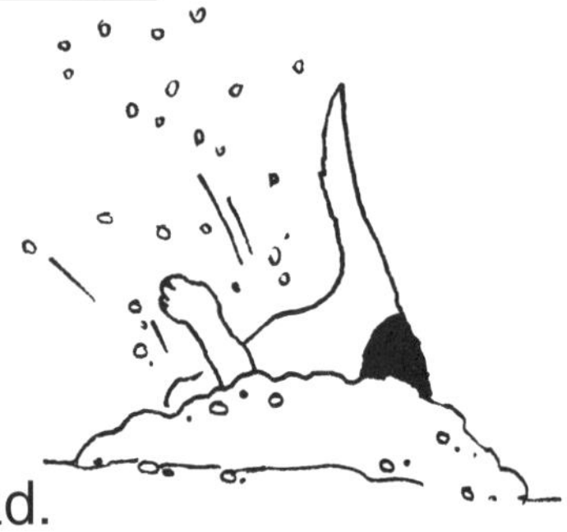

3 Write **list** words in the gaps in these sentences…

The dog ________ a hole in the garden bed.

Did Mum ________ on a race horse on Cup Day ?

The workers dug a big ________ in the middle of the road.

4 These words are written backwards—write them correctly…

p o t s ________ n a r ________ p a g ________

f f o ________ t a p ________ t i p ________

For Fast Finishers

As I was sitting on my chair
I knew the bottom wasn't there,
Nor legs nor back, but I just sat,
Ignoring little things like that.

1 Draw… a stop sign near a deep pit.

2 Finish these Word sums…

d + u + g = ____________ r + i + m = ____________ p + a + t = ____________

b + e + t = ____________ g + a + p = ____________ p + i + t = ____________

3 Which **list** words ?

m i r ____________ f o f ____________ p a g ____________

n r a ____________ b t e ____________ t i p ____________

4 How many **list** words can you find in this Wordsearch ?

S	X	G	A	P
T	V	P	Q	R
O	N	A	B	A
P	I	T	C	N

____________ ____________

____________ ____________

____________ ____________

Classroom Unit 12 c as in cat

Your List

can	cat	cab	cap	cub
cot	cod	cut	cup	cog

1 Tick when you can say…

can	cat	cab	cap
cot	cod	cog	
cut	cub	cup	

2 Copy…

can ____________ cat ____________ cab ____________ cap ____________

cod ____________ cot ____________ cog ____________

cut ____________ cup ____________ cub ____________

3 We are written backwards—write us correctly…

p a c ____________ d o c ____________ g o c ____________

p u c ____________ b u c ____________ n a c ____________

4 Which **list** words… ?

____________ ____________ ____________

5 Write sentences using these words…

cut ____

cot ____

For Fast Finishers

Where are you going,
My little cat?
I am going to town,
To get me a hat.
What! A hat for a cat!
A cat get a hat!
Who ever saw a cat with a hat?

1 Draw…

a cat and a cod in a cab

2 Which words… ?

	o	t
	u	b
	o	g

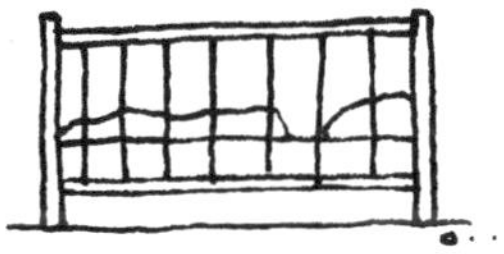

3 Which **list** words are hidden in this Wordfind ?

| c | a | b | c | a | t | n | a | s | c | u | b |

____

____

____

4 Yes or No?

Can a cog swim ? ____________

Can you sleep in a cod ? ____________

Can a cat wear a cap ? ____________

Classroom Unit 13 f as in fan

Your List

fat	fan	fig	fit	fin
fix	fed	fun	fog	fox

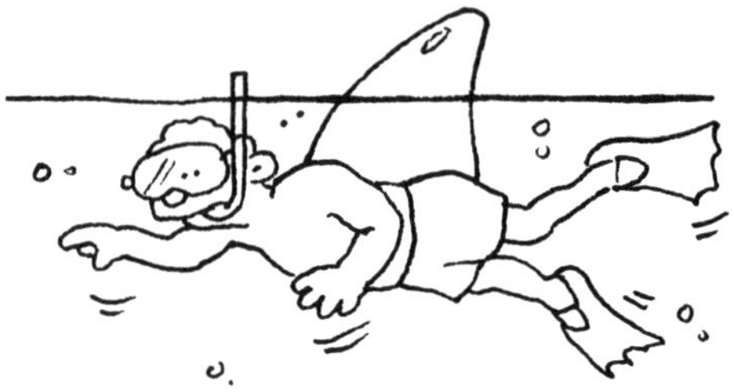

1 Which letters are missing…?

__ a t   f __ d   __ i x   __ u n

2 Draw… a fat fox being fed a fig.

3 Which **list** words best fit into these sentences ?

At the park we had a lot of ______________.

We couldn't see because the ______________ was too thick.

The fish's ______________ cut through the water.

4 Circle the words that match the pictures…

fun
fan
fin

fat
fit
fan

fix
fog
fox

5 Unjumble these **list** words…

g f i ______________   i x f ______________   n u f ______________

For Fast Finishers

To market, to market, to buy fat hog,
Home again, home again, jiggety – jog.

1 Think! Circle the best answer…

I went to market…

… to buy a fat fox.

… to buy a fat home.

… to buy a fat hog.

2 Follow these directions…

Colour the fox red.

Put an X under the fan.

Draw a fin on the fat boy.

3 Finish these Word sums…

f + u + n = ____________ f + i + x = ____________ f + o + g = ____________

f + i + g = ____________ f + o + x = ____________ f + a + n = ____________

4 Which **list** words would fit into this Wordframe…?

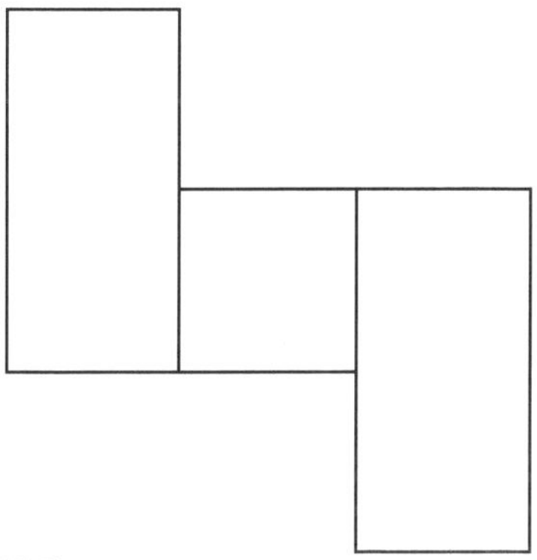

______________ ______________

5 What am I? I help a fish to swim ______________

I mean to have given food ______________

I can keep you cool ______________

Classroom Unit 14 h as in ham

Your List

ham	had	hen	hem	hat
hop	him	hip	hut	hug

1 Copy… ham ________ had ________ hat ________

hen ________ hem ________

hop ________

him ________ hip ________

hut ________ hug ________

2 Which **list** words… ?

________ ________ ________ ________

3 Write words for the pictures in these sentences…

The  ________ ran quickly out of the  ________.

4 Which **list** words are hidden in these bigger words… ?

shop ________ them ________ chimney ________

ship ________ that ________ when ________

5 Tick when you can say…

ham ◯ had ◯ hen ◯ hem ◯

hat ◯ hop ◯ him ◯ hip ◯

hut ◯ hug ◯

For Fast Finishers

Jerry Hall
He is so small,
A rat could eat him,
Hat and all.

1 Which **list** words can you find in these Wordclocks?

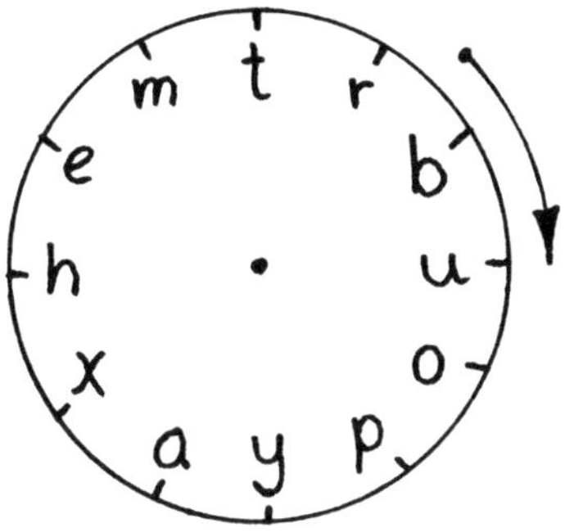

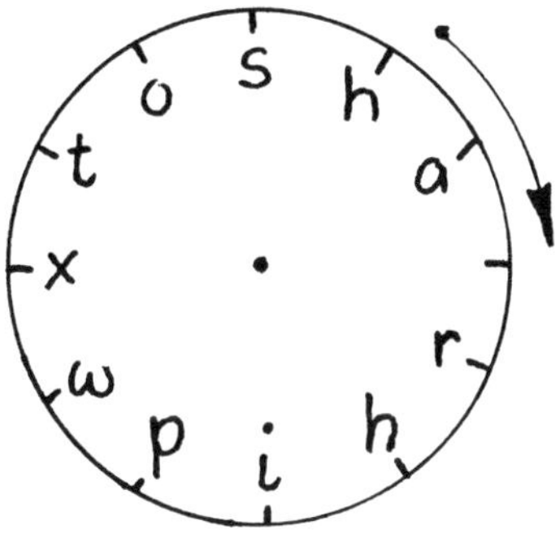

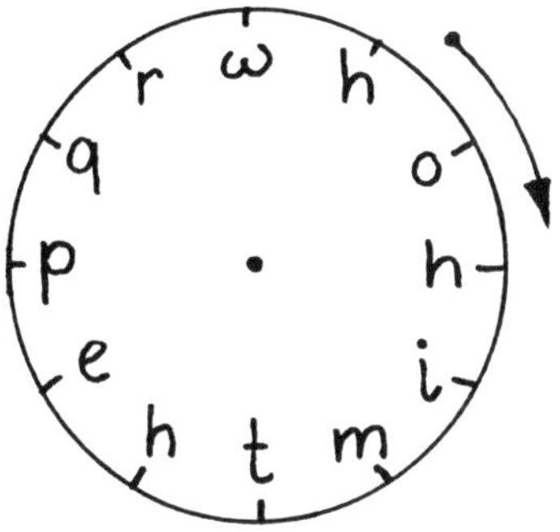

______________ ______________ ______________

2 Draw…

… a hopping hen

… a hat hanging near a hut

3 These **list** words are written backwards—write them correctly…

p i h ______________ m i h ______________ m e h ______________

m a h ______________ p o h ______________ g u h ______________

4 Tick which you think is funny…

A hen had a hat. ◯

He can hop into the hut. ◯

A ham can hug a hut. ◯

Her hem had torn. ◯

Classroom Unit 15 l as in log

Your List

lap	lit	let	leg
lid	log	lot	lip

1 Tick when you can say…

lap ◯

let ◯ leg ◯

lit ◯ lip ◯ lid ◯

log ◯ lot ◯

2 Unjumble these **list** words…

g l o ______ g l e ______ t i l ______

d l i ______ o t l ______ p i l ______

a l p ______ e l t ______

3 Write these **list** words in sentences…

lip ______

log ______

lid ______

4 Look at the word—lit.

What is the first letter? ______ What is the last letter? ______

How many letters are there altogether? ______

What is the middle letter ? ______

5 Which **list** words ?

You can hop, kick or run with me. ______

I come from a tree. ______ I am more than a few. ______

A cat might sit on me when you sit down. ______

For Fast Finishers

Little Tommy Tadpole began to weep and wail,
For Little Tommy Tadpole had lost his little tail,
And his mother didn't know him, as he wept upon a log;
For he wasn't Tommy Tadpole, but Mr Thomas Frog.
(C.J. Dennis)

1 Find the eight **list** words hidden in this Wordsearch…

L	L	N	L	E	T	D	J
A	P	Z	B	F	H	L	L
P	T	W	L	I	P	O	E
V	L	O	T	C	G	G	G
L	I	T	B	L	I	D	K

2 What am I ?

I am on your face. I can be a top or bottom one. When you talk I move.

____

3 Look at the picture. Write Yes or No.

A leg is missing. ______________

A bin is under the log. ______________

A fire has been lit. ______________

A lid is on the bin. ______________

There are a lot of trees. ______________

4 Think! Where did Mr Thomas Frog weep? ____________________________

Classroom Unit 16 m as in man

Your List				
man	map	mug	mud	men
met	mum	mop	mix	me

1 Which **list** words… ?

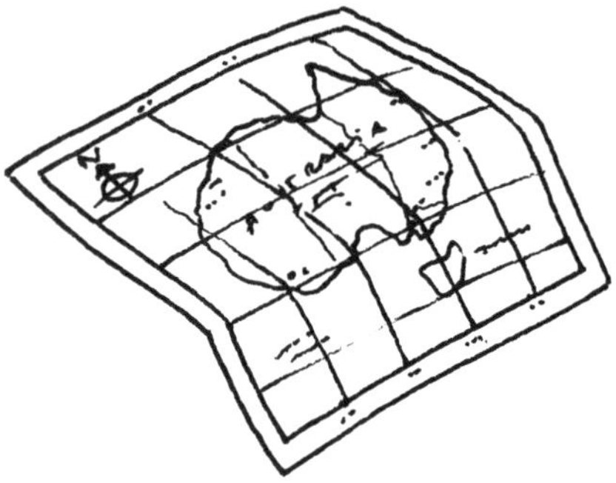

____________ ____________ ____________

2 Write the **list** words which have u as their middle letter.

____________ ____________ ____________

3 Write **list** words in these sentences…

The ____________ mopped up the ____________ .

____________ showed us where we were on the ____________ .

4 Yes or No?

Can a man mix a drink in a mug ? ____________

Can a mop make a map ? ____________

Should you drink mud from a mug ? ____________

5 Unjumble these **list** words…

e m ____________ u m m ____________ i m x ____________

t m e ____________ p a m ____________ m p o ____________

For Fast Finishers

Remember little 'm'
Remember little 'e'
Put them together and
Remember little me.

1 Circle the words that match the pictures…

map
man
mum

mug
mud
mum

me
mop
met

2 Which **list** word is hidden in this Wordfind…?

m	a	g	u	m	u	m	o	t	m	e	r

____

3 Fill in the missing letters…

	o	p
m		g
m	i	
m		n

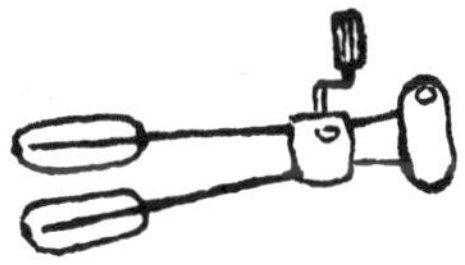

4 Draw a map of the way to your home from school.

Classroom Unit 17 n as in nip

Your List				
net	nip	nan	not	nib
nod	nun	nut	nap	no

1 Tick when you can say…

nan ◯ nap ◯

net ◯

nip ◯ nib ◯

no ◯ not ◯ nod ◯

nut ◯ nun ◯

2 Which **list** words…?

__________ __________ __________

3 Which **list** words rhyme with these…?

pot cot lot __________ rod pod god __________

ban man fan __________ wet get let __________

4 Write a sentence for each of these **list** words…

no ______________________________

not ______________________________

nap ______________________________

5 Which **list** words mean…?

grandmother __________ pen point __________

pinch __________ sleep __________

For Fast Finishers

I had a little nut-tree, nothing would it bear
But a silver nut-meg and a golden pear.

1 How many **list** words can you make…?

ip ap ot ________ ________

n + ________ ________

an et od ________ ________

2 Draw…

… a napping nan

… a netted nun

3 Write the **list** words in this Nonsense word…

napnoonutnipnan ________ ________ ________

________ ________

4 Which is the odd word out…?

net nod not nut ________

nip nib ten nap ________

5 Think! Which **list** words are spelt the same forwards and backwards?

________ ________

Classroom Unit 18 ee as in feed

Your List

seen	feet	feed	tree	weep
deep	seed	been	weed	bee

1 Fill the gaps…

w __ __ p   d __ __ p   f __ __ t   f __ __ d

b __ __ n   s __ __ d   w __ __ d   t r __ __

s __ __ n   b __ __

2 Which **list** words…?

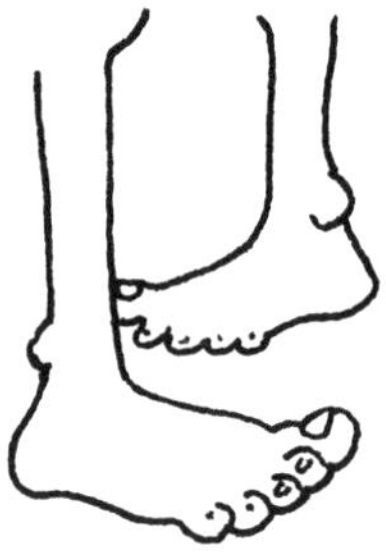

__________ __________ __________ __________

3 Unjumble these **list** words…

d f e e __________   e r t e __________   n e s e __________

e p d e __________   t f e e __________   n e b e __________

4 Write a **list** word in these sentences…

Pussycat, Pussycat where have you __________ ?

At the bottom of your legs are two __________ .

From a tiny __________ a huge __________ grew .

For Fast Finishers

As I sat under the apple tree,
A birdie sent its love to me,
And as I wiped it from my eye,
I said, 'Thank goodness cows can't fly.'

1 Think! Circle the correct answer…

I sat… … in the apple tree.
… behind the apple tree.
… under the apple tree.

A birdie sent its love… … to me.
… from me.
… with me.

2 Draw…

… feet deep in weeds

… a weeping tree

3 Yes or No?

Does a bee have feet? ______________

Can you see a seed on a tree? ______________

Can a tree feed on a bee? ______________

4 Write the **list** words you can see in this picture.

______________ ______________

______________ ______________

______________ ______________

Classroom Review 2

Your List

cab	fin	her	lad	nap
keep	peep	see	week	his

1 Which **list** words… ?

p e p e ______ k e e w ______ s h i ______

b c a ______ n i f ______ p n a ______

2 Write sentences using these **list** words…

keep ______

her ______

lad ______

3 Circle the words that match the pictures…

nap
cab
fin

nap
cab
fin

nap
cab
fin

4 Look at the word—week.

What is the last letter ? ______

What letter comes before k ? ______

What is the third letter ? ______

Which two letters are the same ? ______

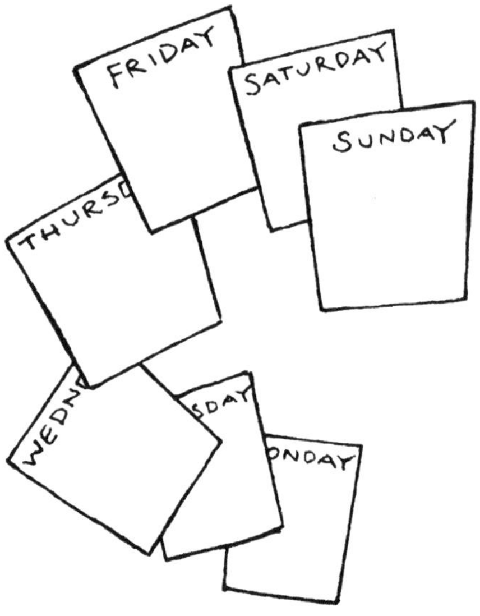

For Fast Finishers

When I look in the mirror

What do I see… ?

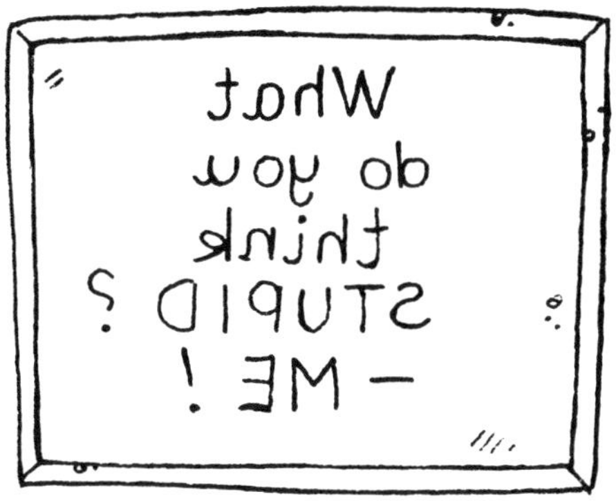

1 Find these **list** words in this Wordsearch…

his	**A**	**S**	**H**	**I**	**S**	**N**
keep	**W**	**E**	**C**	**E**	**T**	**A**
nap	**E**	**E**	**P**	**E**	**E**	**P**
peep	**E**	**V**	**O**	**E**	**N**	**V**
see	**K**	**E**	**E**	**P**	**T**	**W**
week						

2 Finish these Word sums…

p + ee + p = ______________ w + ee + k = ______________

k + ee + p = ______________ c + a + b = ______________

3 Which **list** words fit into these Wordframes…?

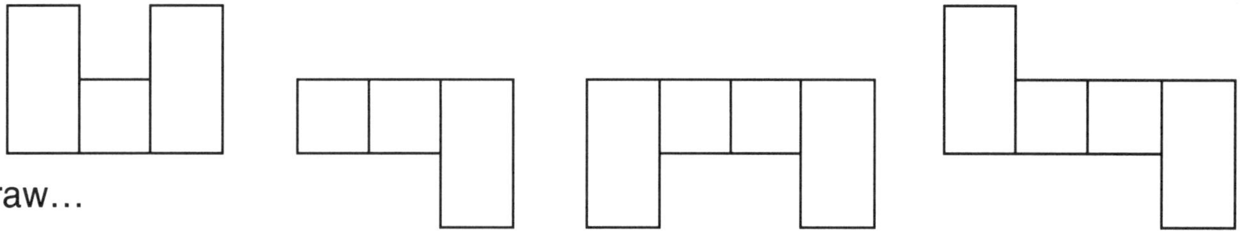

4 Draw…

… two lads (one napping and the other peeping from behind a tree)

Classroom Unit 19 r as in rat

Your List

ram	rat	red	run	rod
rag	rib	rub	rug	rob

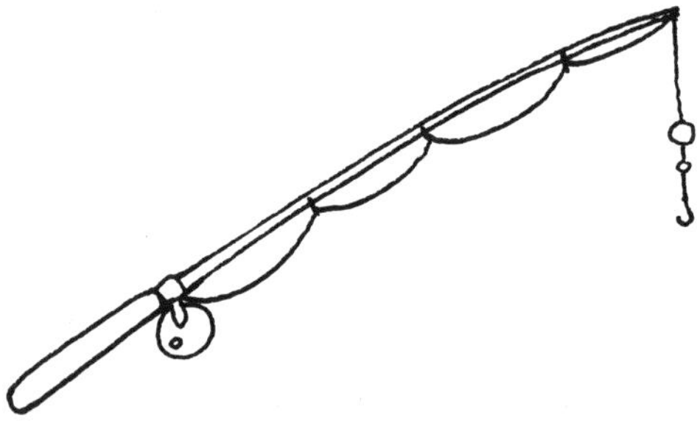

1 Which **list** word am I?

I am a colour. ______________

My meaning is to steal. ______________

You can fish with me. ______________

I am a mat. ______________

I am a male sheep ______________

I am a bone ______________

2 Draw…

… a robber in red rags running from a rat

3 Write the missing letters…

___ a t

___ u n

___ i b

___ a g

___ e d

___ o d

4 Write **list** words in the gaps…

The  ______________ and the  ______________ used

the  ______________ to  ______________ the lamp.

For Fast Finishers

Round and round the ragged rock
The ragged rascal ran
How many R's are there in that ?
Now tell me if you can.

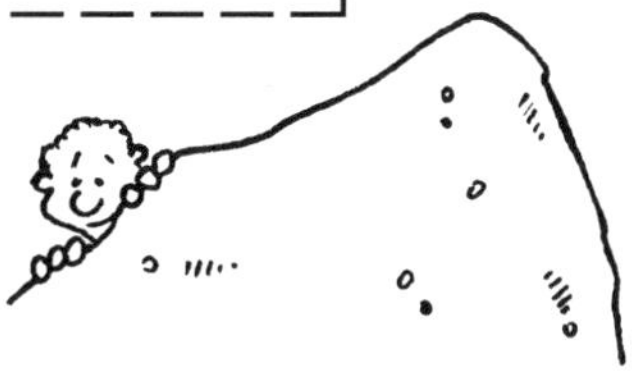

1 Unjumble these **list** words…

b o r ______ b r u ______ u r n ______

g r a ______ t a r ______ a m r ______

2 Finish these Wordcrosses…

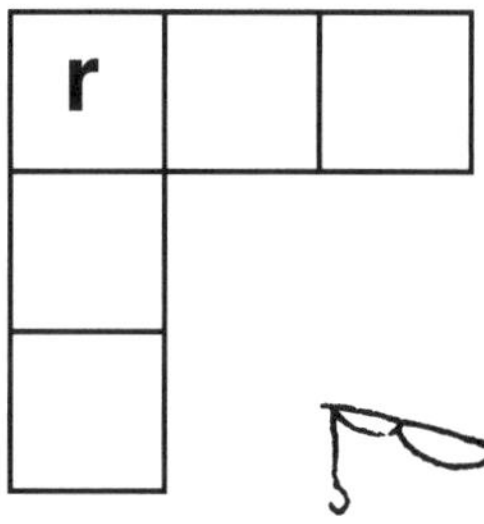

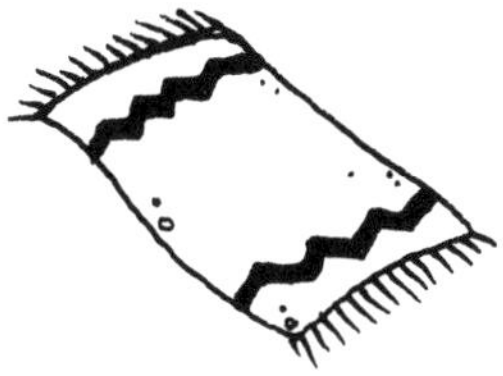

3 Think! Can you answer the riddle in the top corner of this page?

______

4 Which **list** words rhyme with…?

bed ______ pod ______ mob ______

tag ______ ham ______ gun ______

5 Write what you think is happening in this picture.

______

______

______

______

Classroom Unit 20 s as in sat

Your List

sat	sap	sun	sit	sob
six	set	sad	sip	sag

1 Copy…

sat ________ sap ________ sag ________

sad ________ sun ________ set ________

sit ________ six ________ sip ________

sob ________

2 Write a **list** word in these sentences…

The ________ set behind the hill.

The story was so ________ that it made me ________ .

3 Take one letter from these words to make **list** words…

soap = ________ slip = ________ snag = ________

seat = ________ spit = ________ snob = ________

4 Which **list** words…?

____

____

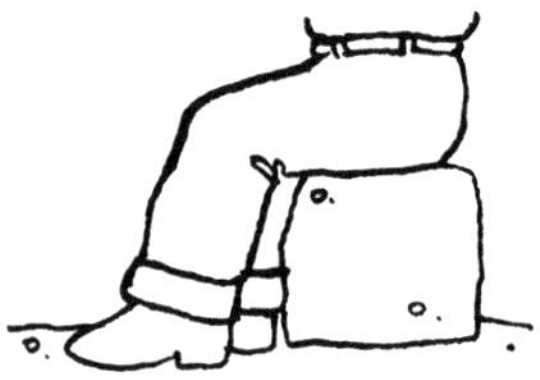

____

5 We are written backwards—write us forwards…

p a s ________ t i s ________ g a s ________

t e s ________ x i s ________ b o s ________

For Fast Finishers

Little Miss Muffet sat on her tuffet,
Eating three Mars Bars a day.
Along came a spider who sat down beside her,
And between them the tuffet gave way.

1 Think! Where did Miss Muffet sit? ______________________________

What did she eat? ______________________________

2 Draw…

… six setting suns

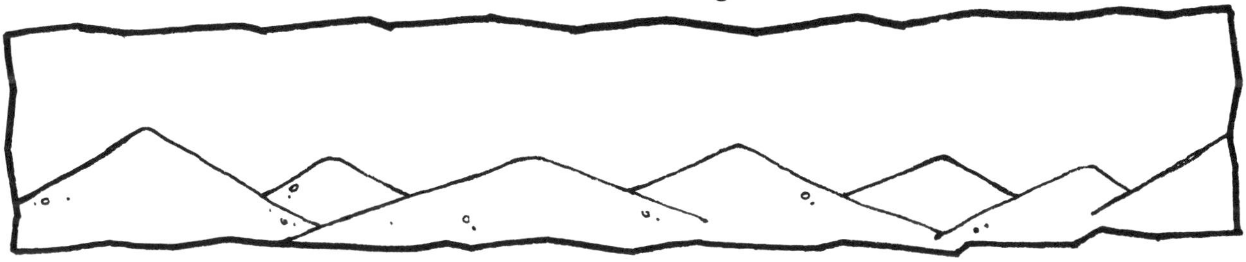

3 Which **list** words…?

I am hot. I am in the sky. I am the ______________ .

I am a number. I am one more than five. I am ______________ .

4 Which **list** word is hidden in this Wordfind…?

s	h	i	s	i	p	s	o	p	s	t	x

____

5 Yes or No?

You may sob if you are sad. ______________

There are six suns in our sky. ______________

You can sip from a tea set. ______________

Classroom Unit 21 v w y as in van wet yes

Your List

van	vet				
wag	wet	wig	web	wax	win
yes	yap				

1 Copy…the **list** words which begin with w.

______ ______ ______ ______

______ ______

2 Which **list** words…?

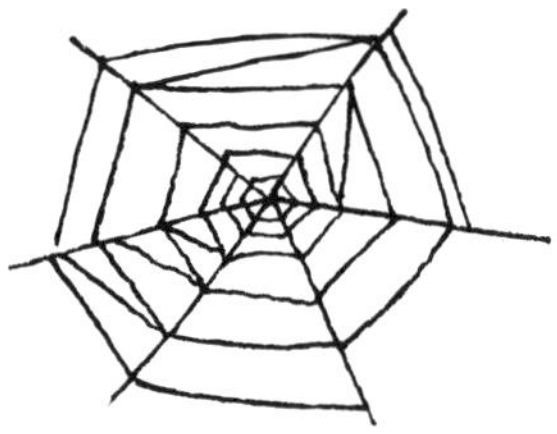

______ ______ ______

3 Which **list** words rhyme with…?

pig ______ gap ______ mess ______

pin ______ sacks ______ sag ______

4 Draw…

…a pig with a wig

…a yapping dog with a wagging tail

5 Write a sentence for each of these words…

vet ______

van ______

For Fast Finishers

Mary, Mary, quite contrary
How does your garden grow ?
With wattle trees, lots of bees,
And funnel webs all in a row.

1 Think! Circle the correct answers…

What grows in Mary's garden…?

bees ◯ vans ◯ trees ◯

spiders ◯ wigs ◯ vets ◯

2 Yes or No?

A dog can wag its tail. ______________ A spider lives in a web. ______________

A wig is made of hot wax. ______________

3 Write the **list** words that you can see in this picture…

(There should be five **list** words.)

______________ ______________ ______________ ______________ ______________

4 How many **list** words can you find in this Wordclock ?

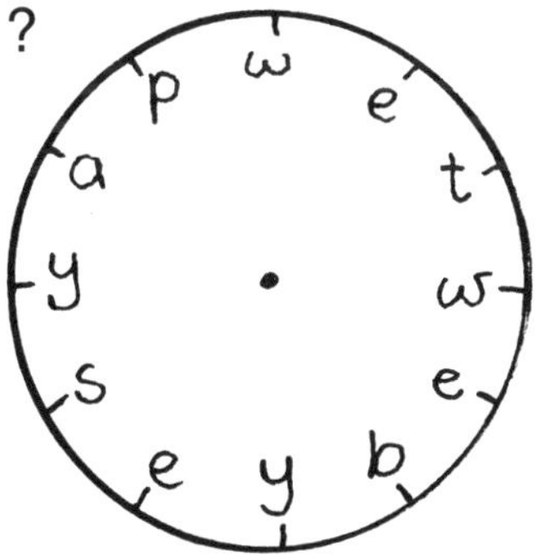

______________ ______________

______________ ______________

Classroom Unit 22 j as in jug

Your List

jam	jet	jug	jog
jab	jig	job	jot

1 Which words…?

	u	**g**
	e	**t**
	a	**m**
	o	**g**

2 We are jumbled. Write us correctly…

g i j ______________ a b j ______________ o j t ______________

3 Yes or No?

Can jam jog ? ______________

Can a jug jot ? ______________

Can you jig when you jog ? ______________

4 Match…

- a dance
- to write quickly
- poke
- work
- run

- job
- jog
- jot
- jab
- jig

For Fast Finishers

Curious fly
Vinegar jug
Slippery edge
Pickled bug

1 Finish these Wordsums…

j + o + t = ____________   j + a + b = ____________

j + a + m = ____________   j + i + g = ____________

2 Can you find all of the **list** words hidden in this Wordsearch? → ↘ ↗ ↓ ↑

C	F	H	J	I	G
D	J	K	J	E	Q
G	A	L	O	P	T
O	B	N	T	R	G
J	A	M	S	U	W
J	O	B	J	V	X

3 Underline all of the **list** words that you can find in this nonsense rhyme…

Jig - a - ty jig
Jog - a - ty jog
Jumbled jam
Said the jumping hog
Jab - a - ty jab
Jug - a - ty jig
Just the job
Said the jaunty pig.

4 Fill in the missing letters…

j __ m   __ o b   j u __   j __ t

Classroom Unit 23 k as in kit

Your List
kit kid kin keg kiss

1 Copy…

kit ______________ kid ______________ keg ______________

kiss ______________ kin ______________

2 Which **list** words…?

______________ ______________ ______________ ______________

3 We are written backwards—write us correctly…

n i k ______________ t i k ______________ s s i k ______________

4 Which **list** words would fit into these Wordframes…?

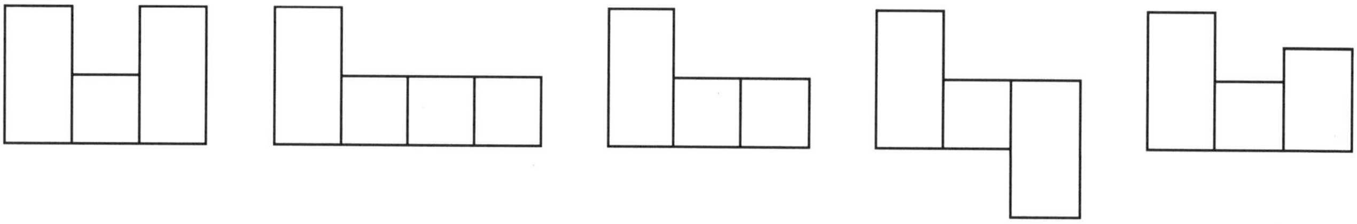

5 Write the missing letters…

k __ g k __ t k __ n

k __ d k __ s __

6 Write a **list** word in the gap in this sentence…

The worker packed her tool ______________ into a small red box.

For Fast Finishers

There's too many kids in this tub
There's too many elbows to scrub.
I just washed a behind
That I'm sure wasn't mine—
There's too many kids in this tub.
(Shel Silverstein)

1 Think! Which **list** words belong to these groups…?

billy-goat nanny-goat ______________

aunt uncle cousin ______________

barrel cask ______________

2 Which **list** words are hidden in these larger words…?

skid ______________ kitten ______________ skinny ______________

3 Finish this Wordcross…

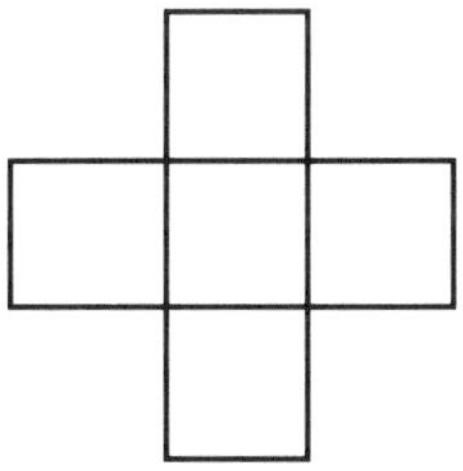

Down: a young goat (or child)

Across: your relatives

4 Which **list** words rhyme with…?

win ______________ miss ______________ lid ______________

pit ______________ peg ______________

5 Draw…kissing kids.

Classroom Unit 24 all as in ball

Your List

ball	tall	fall
call	wall	hall

1 Copy…

hall __________ fall __________ call __________

wall __________ ball __________ tall __________

2 Which **list** words…?

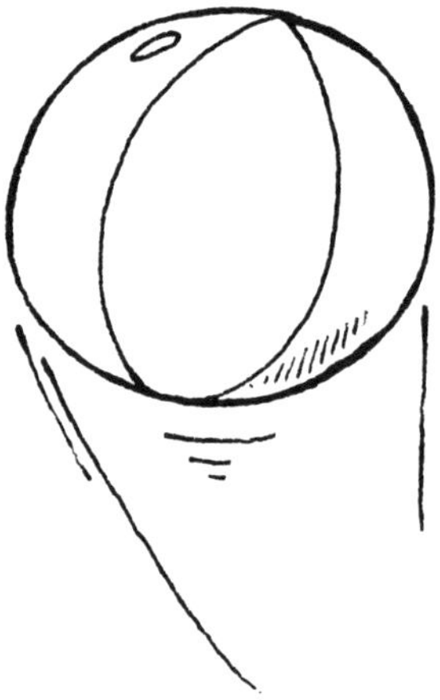

__________ __________ __________

3 Write each of these **list** words in a sentence…

hall ______________________________

fall ______________________________

call ______________________________

4 We are jumbled up—write us correctly…

l t l a __________ a h l l __________ l a c l __________

b l a l __________ l l a w __________ l f a l __________

For Fast Finishers

Humpty Dumpty sat on a wall,
Humpty Dumpty had a great fall,
All the King's horses and all the King's men,
Had scrambled eggs for breakfast again.

1 Think !

Where was Humpty Dumpty sitting…?

…in a hall
…on a ball
…on a wall

Humpty Dumpty…

…had a ball
…had a fall
…was tall

2 Add together to make **list** words…

(t) (w) (b) (f) (c) + all = ______________ ______________ ______________ ______________ ______________

Which word is missing ? ______________

3 Draw…

…a falling ball

…a tall wall

4 Which **list** words are hidden in this Wordfind…?

l	c	a	l	l	t	a	l	l	f	a	l	l	b	a

______________ ______________ ______________

Classroom Unit 25 ell as in bell

Your List

bell fell sell tell well yell

1 Copy…

bell ______ fell ______ tell ______

sell ______ well ______ yell ______

2 Which **list** words…?

______ ______ ______

3 Write each of these **list** words in a sentence…

well ______

yell ______

bell ______

4 Which **list** words…?

My first letter is **s**. ______

I begin with the second letter of the alphabet. ______

I begin with the second last letter of the alphabet. ______

5 Which words mean…?

not sick ______ call loudly ______ to say ______

For Fast Finishers

It doesn't breathe;
It doesn't smell;
It doesn't feel so very well.
I am disgusted with my nose.
The only thing it does is blows.

1 Think! Which **list** words do you think come from these...?

fall ______________ told ______________ sold ______________

2 Which word fits best...?

You can ring me.	fell	bell	well
I am a loud call.	yell	sell	tell
I mean good health.	bell	tell	well
I mean to exchange for money.	well	sell	fell

3 Find all of the **list** words in this Wordsearch.

You may find the words ↓ ↑ → ↘ ↗

E	H	I	W	Y	E	L	L	P	Q
L	B	G	J	E	L	L	O	F	T
A	E	C	T	E	L	M	N	E	U
D	L	F	T	B	K	L	R	L	V
B	L	E	S	E	L	L	S	L	W

4 Read this story and then answer the questions...

A man who was trying to sell umbrellas fell into a well.
We rang an alarm bell. We could not tell if he was well until we heard him yell that he was all right.

Was the man well after he fell into the well ? ______________

What was the man trying to sell ? ______________

Which came first...an alarm bell, a yell or a fall? ______________

Classroom Unit 26 ll as in bill ull as in bull

Your List

bill fill hill kill mill pill will
bull full pull

1 Copy…

bill ________ bull ________ fill ________ full ________

pill ________ pull ________ hill ________ kill ________

mill ________ will ________

2 We are jumbled—write us correctly…

l i k l ________ u l f l ________ l i p l ________

w i l i ________ l u l b ________ l l u p ________

3 Circle the words that match the pictures…

bill

bull

pull

fill

will

hill

4 Which **list** words are hidden in these larger words…?

bullet ________ pulley ________ skill ________

spoonbill ________ chilly ________ windmill ________

5 Draw… a windmill on top of a hill

For Fast Finishers

There was an old woman
Lived under a hill,
And if she's not gone
She lives there still.

1 Think!

The old woman lived… …on a hill.
…in a hill.
…under a hill.

2 Which three **list** words are hidden in this Wordclock?

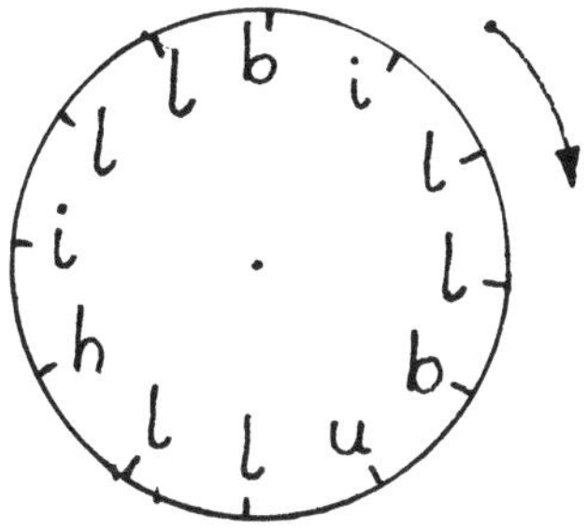

____

____

____

3 Write the **list** words which begin with **b**. ______________ ______________

4 Which **list** word means not empty? ______________

5 Write the **list** words which begin with **f**. ______________ ______________

6 What is happening? Write what is happening in this picture.

____

____

____

Classroom Review 3

Your List

ran	sum	van	well	yet
just	kill	wall	pull	yell

1 Copy…

ran ______ sum ______ yet ______

just ______ kill ______ van ______

well ______ pull ______ wall ______

yell ______

2 Tick when you can say…

ran ○ sum ○ van ○ yet ○ pull ○

well ○ yell ○ kill ○ just ○ wall ○

3 Which **list** words…?

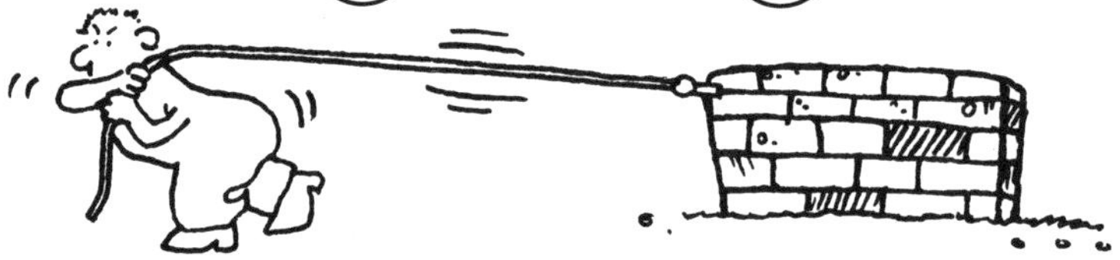

4 + 2 + 6

______ ______ ______

4 Write sentences using these **list** words…

just ______

ran ______

yet ______

5 Which **list** words rhyme with these…?

full ______ must ______ come ______

vet ______ smell ______ ______

fan ______ ______

For Fast Finishers

A doctor fell into a well
And broke his collarbone,
A doctor should attend the sick
And leave the well alone.

1 Which word…?

8 + 1 = 9 sum or some

2 Draw…just a wall

3 Follow the letter path

On the way, write down any **list** words you can find. There should be six.

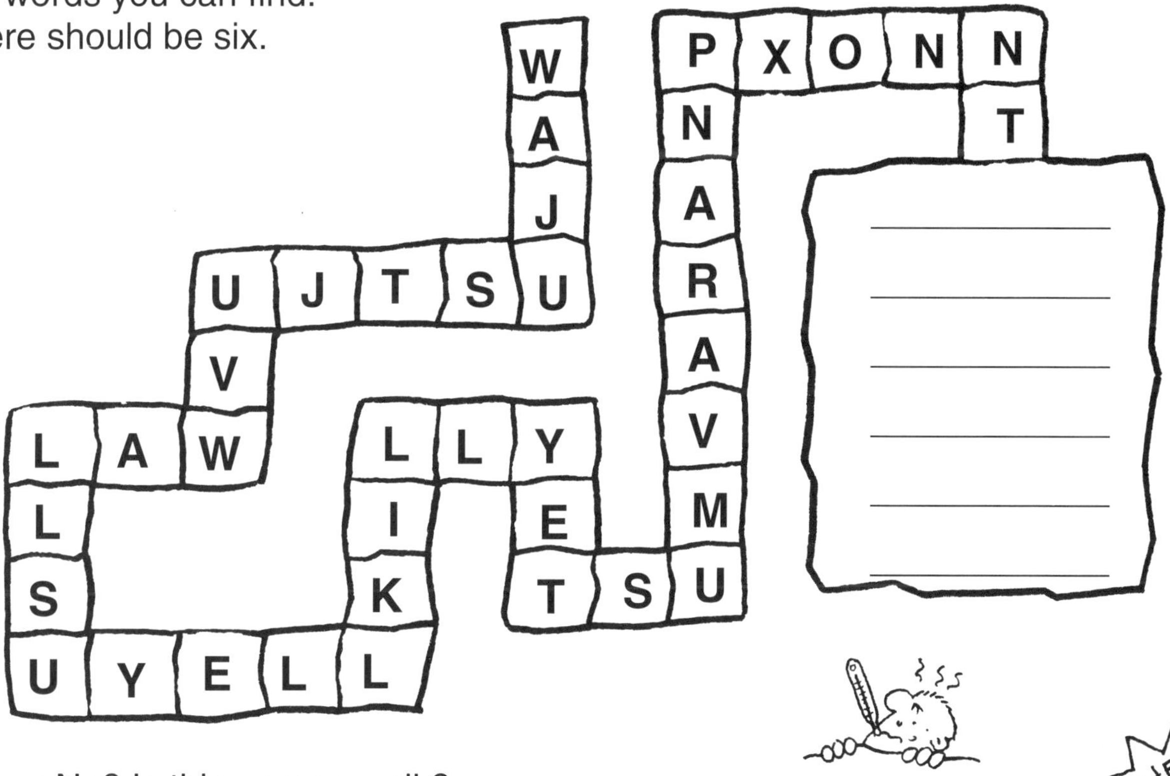

4 Yes or No? Is this person well ? ______________

Is the yell coming from behind the wall ? ______________

Is this sum correct? ______________ 2 + 2 + 2 = 8

Classroom Unit 27 ch as in chop

Your List
chat chin chop chap chess

1 Copy… chat ______________ chip ______________

chin ______________ chop ______________

chap ______________ chess ______________

2 Tick when you can say…

chap ◯ chip ◯ chin ◯ chop ◯ chap ◯ chess ◯

3 Write **list** words in the gaps in these sentences…

The woodcutter used an axe to ______________ the tree down.

The giant grew a big black beard on the point of his ______________ .

This cup has a ______________ in it .

4 Which **list** words…?

______________ ______________ ______________

5 What am I? I am friendly talk. c h __ __

I am a bony slice of meat. c h __ __

I am a game. c h __ __ __

For Fast Finishers

Flippity-flop! Flippity-flop!

Here comes the butcher to bring us a chop.

1 Think! What will the butcher bring?

____

2 Draw… a chap chopping (show some wood chips in your picture).

3 Which **list** words rhyme with these…?

fin __________ stop __________ bat __________

mess __________ sip __________ map __________

4 Which **list** words are hidden in these Wordclocks ?

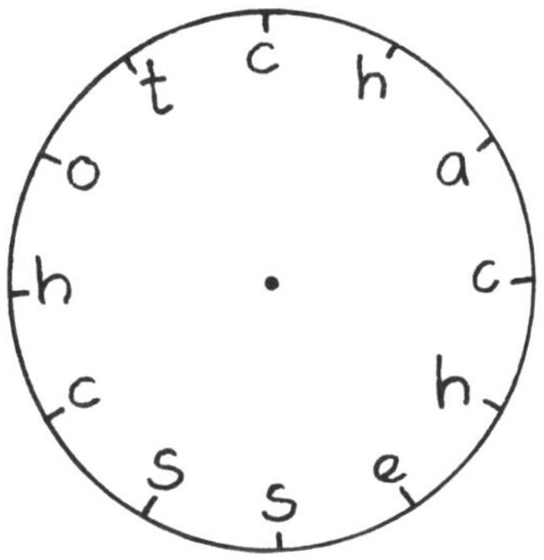

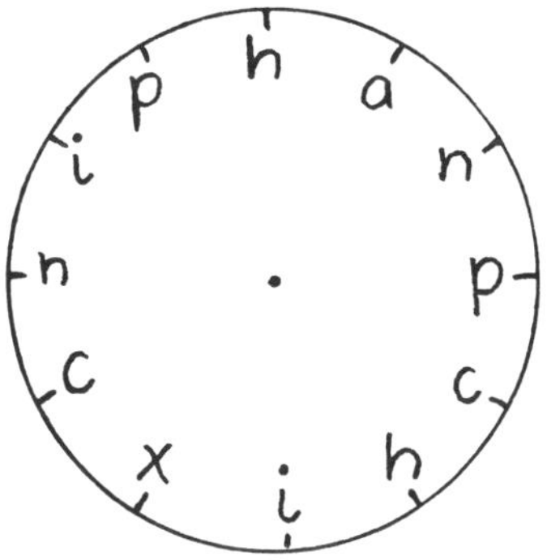

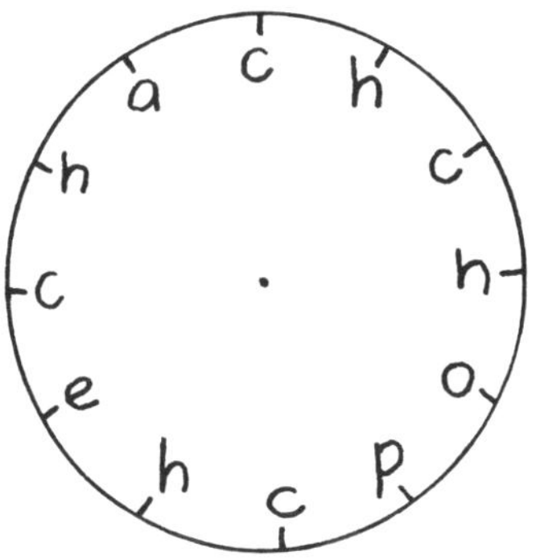

__________ __________ __________

Classroom Unit 28 sh as in shed

Your List

shop	shot	shed	ship
shut	shin	shell	she

1 Copy…

she ____________ shell ____________ shed ____________ shop ____________

shot ____________ ship ____________ shin ____________ shut ____________

2 Tick when you can say…

she ◯ shed ◯ shell ◯

shin ◯ ship ◯

shop ◯ shot ◯

shut ◯

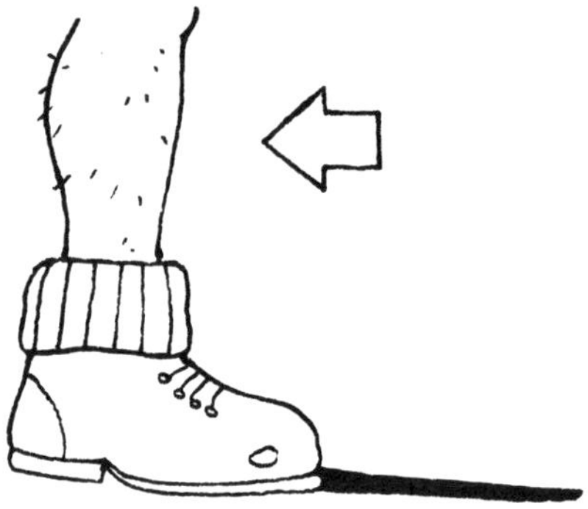

3 Circle the words that match the pictures…

shin
ship
shot

shed
shot
shin

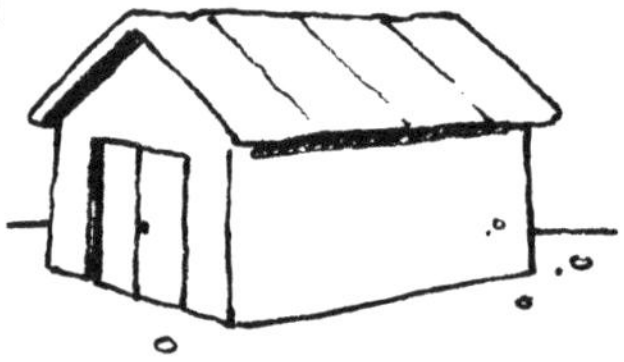

shed
she
shell

4 Yes or No?

A shin is on your leg. ____________

All shops are really sheds. ____________

Ships sail on the sea. ____________

5 Write sentences using these **list** words…

she ____

shot ____

6 Write the missing letters…

__ __ o p   __ __ o t   __ __ e d   __ __ e l l

For Fast Finishers

The rain is raining all around,
It falls on field and tree;
It rains on the umbrellas here,
And on the ships at sea.
(R.L. Stevenson)

1 Think! Tick the best answers…

The rain is falling… on fields ___ on ships ___ on shops ___

on people ___ on dogs ___ on trees ___ on umbrellas ___

2 Write the **list** words hidden in these larger words…

shoppers ____________ shutters ____________ shopping ____________

township ____________ gunshot ____________ shellfish ____________

3 Finish these Word sums…

sh + o + t = ______________ sh + o + p = ______________

sh + e + ll = ______________ sh + u + t = ______________

sh + i + n = ______________ sh + i + p = ______________

4 Which **list** words are hiding these smaller words…?

hot __ __ __ __ hut __ __ __ __ hip __ __ __ __

hop __ __ __ __ he __ __ __

5 What is happening? Write what you think is happening in this picture.

____

____

____

____

Classroom Unit 29 sl as in slap

Your List
slap slab slam sled slip
slim slit slot slug slop

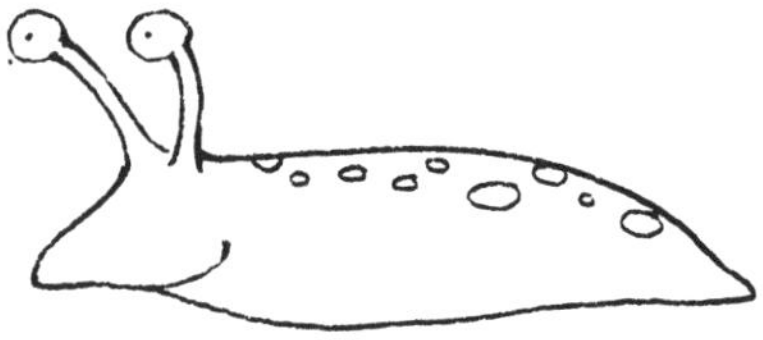

1 Copy…

slab ________ slam ________ slap ________

sled ________ slim ________ slip ________

slit ________ slop ________ slot ________

slug ________

2 Tick when you can say…

slab ◯ slam ◯ slap ◯ sled ◯ slim ◯

slip ◯ slit ◯ slop ◯ slot ◯ slug ◯

3 Which **list** word am I…?

I am thin. ________

I slide on snow. ________

I am a slimy animal. ________

4 Use **list** words to finish these sentences…

Please don't ________ the door.

Clap your hands and then ________ your knees.

Bob cut us all a large ________ of cake.

5 We are written backwards—write us correctly…

m a l s ________ m i l s ________ t i l s ________

t o l s ________ p i l s ________ p o l s ________

For Fast Finishers

Down the slippery slide they slid,
Sitting slightly sideways,
Slipping swiftly, see them skid
On holidays and Fridays.

1 Think! When do they slide down the slippery slide?

____

2 Write down any five of the **list** words and try to say them aloud quickly.

__________ __________ __________ __________ __________

You have made your own **Tongue Twister**. Make another by changing the words.

__________ __________ __________ __________ __________

3 Follow this Wordslide—how many **list** words can you find ?

____

____

____

____

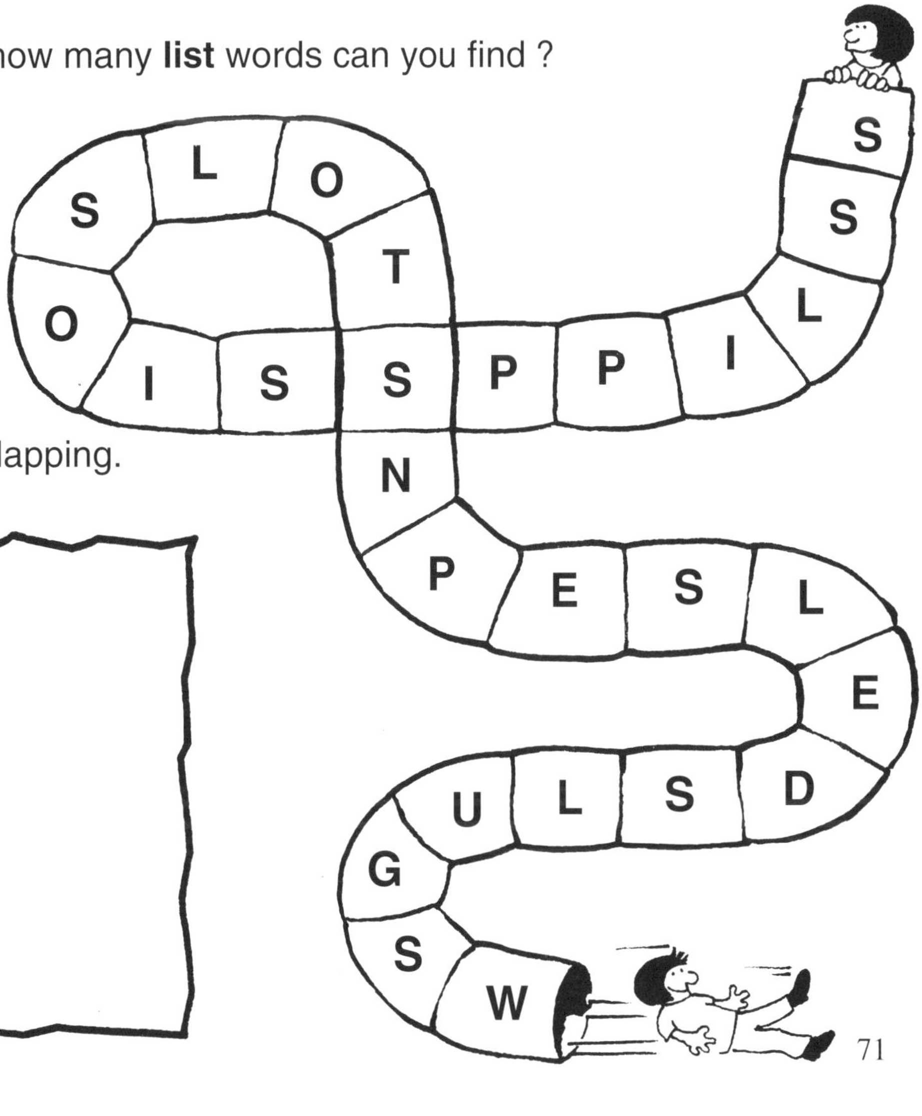

4 Draw…a slug slip slop slapping.

Classroom Unit 30 sm as in smog sn as in snap

Your List
smog small smell
snip snap snag snug snob

1 Copy… small ________ smell ________

smog ________ snag ________ snap ________

snip ________ snob ________ snug ________

2 Tick when you can say…

small ◯ smell ◯ smog ◯

snag ◯ snap ◯

snip ◯ snug ◯ snob ◯

3 Write the missing letters…

__ __ a g __ __ o g __ __ e l l

__ __ ap __ __ a l l __ __ o b

4 Which **list** words…?

s n __ __

s n __ __

s m __ __ __

5 What am I? I am a dirty cloud. ________

I am warm and comfortable. ________

I am a small cut. ________

For Fast Finishers

Mary had a little lamb,
As dirty as a hog,
They asked her how it got that way,
She answered simply, 'Smog.'

1 Which **list** words fit into this Wordcross...?

2 Write each of these **list** words in sentences...

snag ______________________________

snip ______________________________

small ______________________________

3 Think! Why was Mary's lamb dirty? ______________________

4 Unjumble these **list** words...

l s m l e ____________ b o n s ____________

g u n s ____________ p i n s ____________

5 Finish these Word sums...

sm + a + ll = ____________ sm + e + ll = ____________

sn + u + g = ____________ sn + a + g = ____________

sm + o + g = ____________ sn + i + p = ____________

Classroom Unit 31 sp as in spin

Your List

spin	spot	spit	span
spy	speed	spell	spill

1 Copy…

span ______________ speed ______________ spell ______________

spill ______________ spin ______________ spy ______________

spit ______________ spot ______________

2 Tick when you can say…

span ◯ speed ◯ spell ◯ spill ◯

spin ◯ spit ◯ spot ◯ spy ◯

3 Write **list** words in the gaps in these sentences…

'______________ out the water into the bowl', said the dentist.

The witch cast a magic ______________ .

If you ______________ the top it will go around and around.

4 Which **list** words…?

______________ ______________ ______________

For Fast Finishers

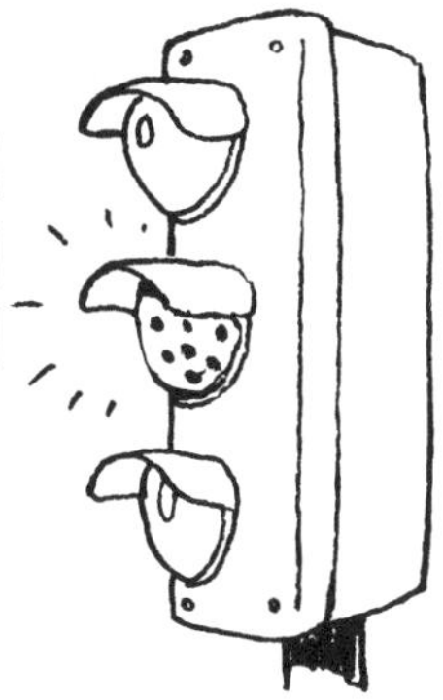

When the light is green you go.
When the light is red you stop.
But what do you do
When the light turns blue
With orange and lavender spots?
(Shel Silverstein)

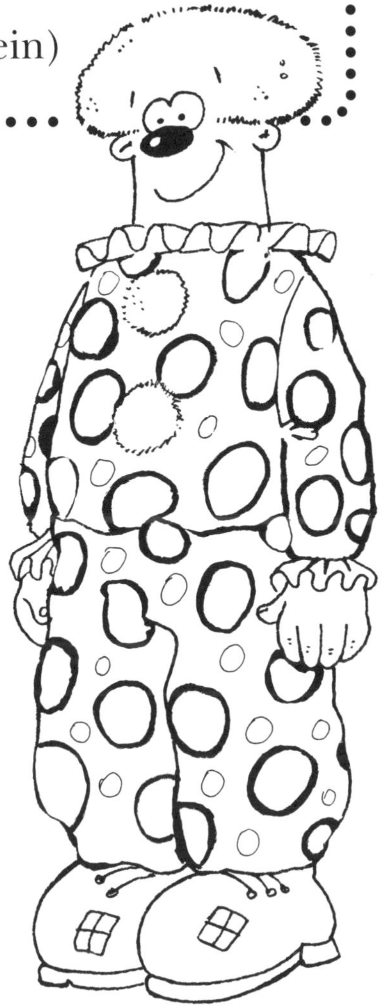

1 Think ! What do you do…?

…when the light is green ? ______________

…when the light is red ? ______________

2 Colour the large spots yellow.
Colour the small spots pink.

3 I spy with my little eye!
How many things, beginning with **sp** do you spy in this picture?

____

____

____

____

____

Classroom Unit 32 st as in stop

Your List

stop	stab	stem	step	stun
stay	stub	steep	still	stall

1 Copy…

stab ______ stag ______ stall ______

steep ______ stem ______ step ______

still ______ stop ______

stub ______ stun ______

2 Tick when you can say…

stab ◯ stag ◯ stall ◯ steep ◯

stem ◯ step ◯ stun ◯ stub ◯

stop ◯ still ◯

3 Which **list** words…?

______ ______ ______

4 These words are backwards—write them correctly…

l l a t s ______ n u t s ______ b u t s ______

g a t s ______ p o t s ______ p e e t s ______

5 Write the missing letters…

__ __ a b   __ __ u n   s t __ __ p   s t a __ __

For Fast Finishers

1 Think! Colour the stair where I always stop.

2 Look at the word **steep**.

Which letter is first ? ______________

Which letter is second ? ______________

Which letter is doubled ? ______________

Which letter is last ? ______________

3 Draw… …a stunned stag (a stag is a deer).

4 Find the **list** words in this Wordsearch…

The words can be found ↓ → ↘ ↗

S	T	S	T	A	L	L	S
O	S	T	T	A	B	B	T
X	T	E	C	E	U	D	O
S	I	E	E	T	M	F	P
T	L	P	S	T	U	N	Y
A	L	G	H	I	J	A	K
B	L	M	N	K	T	Q	S
S	T	E	P	S	P	R	T

Halfway down the stairs
Is a stair
Where I sit.
There isn't any
Other stair
Quite like
It.
I'm not at the bottom;
I'm not at the top;
So this is the stair
Where
I always
Stop.

(A.A. Milne)

Classroom Unit 33 sw as in swim

Your List
swag swim swan sweep sweet swell

1 Copy…

swag ______ swan ______ swim ______

sweet ______ sweep ______ swell ______

2 Tick when you can say…

swag ◯ swan ◯ swim ◯ sweep ◯

sweet ◯ swell ◯

3 Write a sentence for each word…

swim ______

sweet ______

sweep ______

4 Which **list** words…?

I am a bird ______

To move in the water ______

A bed roll ______

5 Circle the words that match the pictures…

sweep
sweet
swell

sweep
sweet
swell

sweep
sweet
swell

6 Write the **list** words which have these smaller words in them…

weep ______ well ______ wag ______

For Fast Finishers

Swan swam over the sea,
Swim, swan, swim!
Swan swam back again,
Well swum, swan!

1 Think! Which **list** words best go with these…?

a swagman ____________ a lolly ____________

backstroke ____________ a waterbird ____________

a broom ____________ a balloon ____________

2 There are three **list** words hidden in this Wordclock—write them in the spaces.

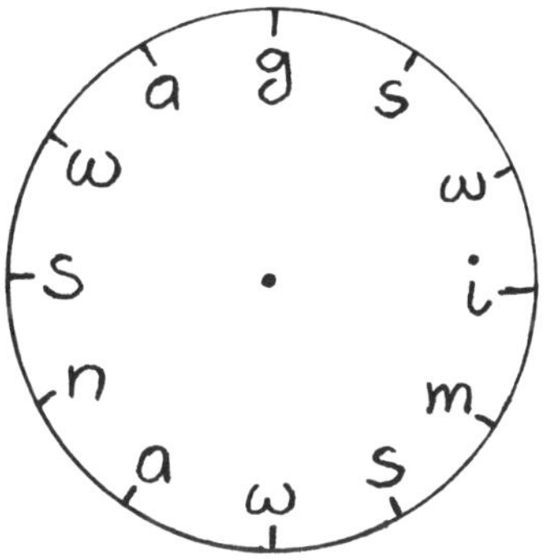

____

____

____

3 Unjumble us to find the six **list** words…

l e w l s ____________ n s a w ____________ g w s a ____________

p s e e w ____________ t w s e e ____________ m s w i ____________

4 Look at the picture…

Colour the swag yellow.

Colour the swan black.

Colour the swimmer red.

Colour the sweeper green.

Classroom Unit 34 mp as in lamp

Your List

lamp camp damp ramp limp
lump jump pump bump hump

1 Copy…

camp ______ damp ______ lamp ______

ramp ______ limp ______ bump ______

hump ______ jump ______ lump ______

pump ______

2 Tick when you can say…

camp ○ damp ○ lamp ○ ramp ○

limp ○

bump ○ hump ○ jump ○ lump ○ pump ○

3 Which **list** words…?

  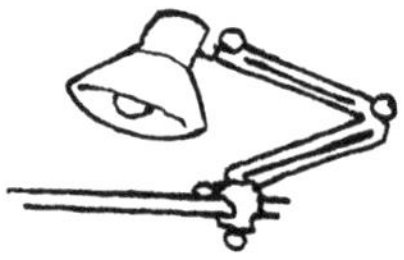 

______ ______ ______ ______

4 Yes or No? A camp can jump. ______

A camel has a hump. ______

5 Which **list** words can you make by joining these groups ?

d l c r	+	a i u	+	mp

______ ______

______ ______

______

For Fast Finishers

Here's a joke to tell your mum,
It certainly will stump her:
If you cross a sheep and a kangaroo
You get…a woolly jumper.

1 Think!

What do you get if you cross a sheep and a kangaroo? ______________

2 Which **list** words match these pictures…?

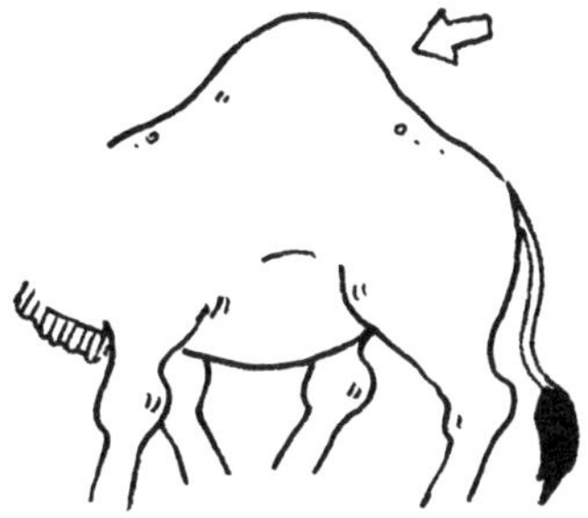

______________ ______________ ______________ ______________

3 Draw…a camel, with two humps, jumping from a ramp.

4 Which **list** words would fit into this Wordframe ?

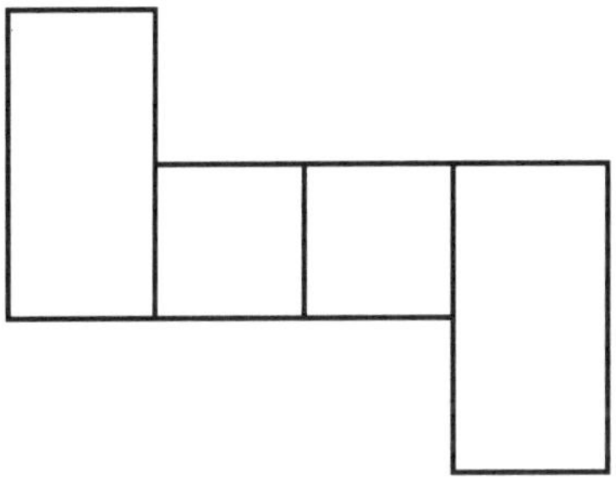

______________ ______________ ______________

______________ ______________ ______________

5 Write the missing letters…

c a __ __   r a __ __   l u __ __

j __ __ p   p __ __ p   d __ __ p

Classroom Unit 35 ar as in car

Your List

car jar bar tar far star

1 Copy…

bar ______ car ______ far ______

jar ______ star ______ tar ______

2 Tick when you can say…

bar ◯ car ◯ far ◯ jar ◯ star ◯ tar ◯

3 Which **list** words are hidden in these larger words…?

starlight ______ carpet ______ target ______

faraway ______ barber ______ carnival ______

4 Yes or No?

A star is far away. ______

A car is kept in a jar. ______

You can break up tar with a strong bar. ______

5 We are jumbled—write us correctly…

a r c ______ t r a s ______ r a t ______

a b r ______ a j r ______ f r a ______

6 Write these words in sentences…

car ______

far ______

For Fast Finishers

Starlight, star bright,
First star I see tonight,
I wish I may, I wish I might—
Oh, rats, it's just a satellite.

1 Think!

Can you unjumble the word rats to find a **list** word? ______________

2 Which **list** words are hidden in this Wordfind…?

b	r	f	r	a	a	j	a	r	c	r	c	a	r	b	f	b	a	r	a

______________ ______________ ______________

3 Which **list** words best fit these pictures…?

car
star
tar

bar
jar
far

tar
bar
car

4 Write the missing letters in this Crossword…

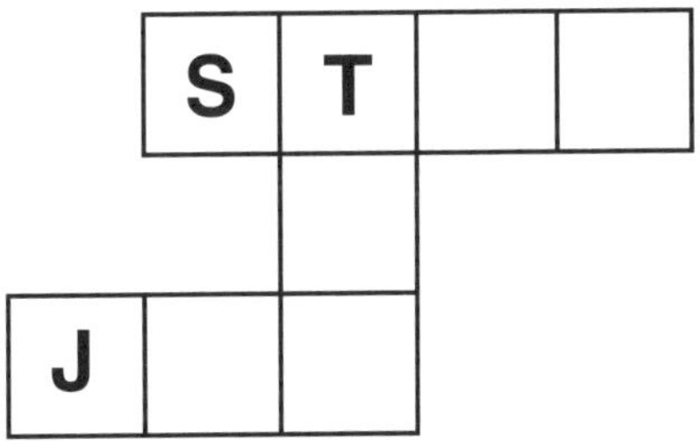

5 Write the **list** words in the correct Wordframes…

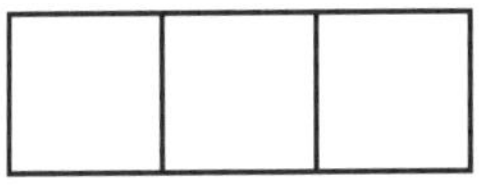

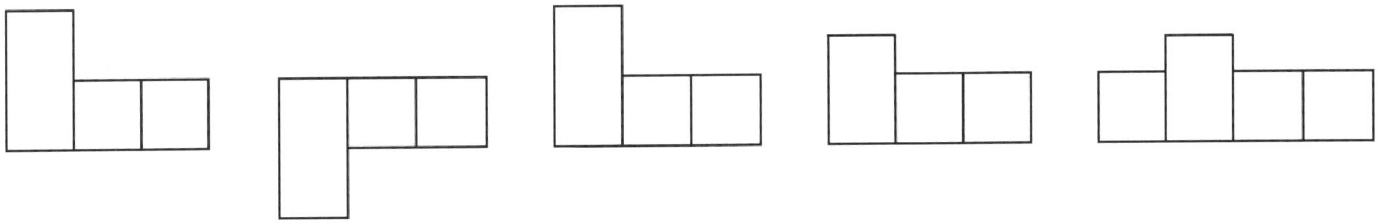

Classroom Unit 36 ay as in day

Your List

day	way	hay	ray	play	stay
say	bay	pay	tray	today	

1 Complete…

Night comes before ______________ .

The cups are on the ______________ .

Which ______________ should we go?

2 Draw… children playing in the hay on a sunny day.

3 These words are backwards—write them correctly…

y a r ______________ y a w ______________

y a h ______________ y a b ______________

4 Write the first letter of each word in the boxes…

today ☐ play ☐ tray ☐

5 Write a sentence with each of these words…

today ____

say ____

6 Write the last letter of each word in the box…

stay ☐ hay ☐ bay ☐

For Fast Finishers

Each morning, as I lie in bed,
The sun comes streaming round my head,
And wakes me up, and seems to say,
'Here comes another happy day.'
(Lydia Pender)

1 Think! What does the sun seem to say?

____

2 Which **list** word is hidden in this Wordsearch?

____

S	A	S	O	Y
Y	O	T	A	U
P	X	A	V	P
Z	A	Y	R	N

3 Draw…something you might find in a playground.

4 What am I ?

I am dry grass __ __ __   I am this day __ __ __ __ __

5 Finish these Word sums…

r + a + y = __________   st + a + y = __________   w + a + y = __________

Classroom Review 4

Your List

chill	shell	slip	snap	small
spell	star	stamp	sway	dump

1 Copy…

chill ______________ dump ______________ shell ______________

slip ______________ small ______________ snap ______________

spell ______________ stamp ______________ star ______________

sway ______________

2 Tick when you can say…

chill ◯ dump ◯ shell ◯ slip ◯

small ◯ snap ◯ spell ◯ stamp ◯

star ◯ sway ◯

3 Which **list** word…?

______________ ______________ ______________

4 Write a **list** word in the gaps in these sentences…

If you go outside in winter you may catch a ______________ .

When the wind is strong, the trees ______________ backwards and forwards.

The witch cast a ______________ .

5 Write the first two letters of each of these words…

shell __ __ slip __ __ small __ __ snap __ __

spell __ __ star __ __ stamp __ __ sway __ __

6 Write the last two letters of each of these words…

dump __ __ stamp __ __ chill __ __ small __ __

spell __ __ shell __ __

For Fast Finishers

Pip Pip Pippety Pip
Slid on the lino
Slippety slip
Fell down the stairs
Trippety trip
Tore her pants
Rippety rip
Started to cry
Drippety drip
Poor little Pippa
Pippety Pip !

1 Think!

Tick which Pippa did first…

…tore her pants ◯

…started to cry ◯

…slid on the lino ◯

2 Which words…?

	P		**L**	
	D			**P**
C			**L**	
S	**H**			
	S			**Y**

3 Draw… a small star-shaped shell.

4 Which **list** words are hiding these smaller words…?

way ____________ lip ____________ hill ____________

am ____________ tar ____________ all ____________

Your Spelling Words

B
bad
bag
ball
bar
bat
bay
bed
bee
been
bell
bet
big
bill
bin
box
bull
bump
bun
bus
but

C
cab
call
camp
can
cap
car
cat
chap
chat
chess
chill
chin
chop
cod
cog
cot
cub
cup
cut

D
dad
dam
damp
day
deep
den
did
dig
dim
dip
do
dog
dot
dug
dump

F
fall
fan
far
fat
fed
feed
feet
fell
fig
fill
fin
fit
fix
fog
fox
full
fun

G
gap
gas
get
go
god
got
gum
gun

H
had
hall
ham
hat
hay
hem
hen
her
hill
him
hip
his
hit
hop
hot
hug
hump
hut

I
in

J
jab
jam
jar
jet
jig
job
jog
jot
jump
jug
just

K
keg
keep
kid
kill
kin
kiss
kit

Your Spelling Words

L
lad
lamp
lap
leg
let
lid
limp
lip
lit
log
lot
lump

M
man
map
mat
me
men
met
mill
mix
mop
mud
mug
mum

N
nan
nap
net
nib
nip
no
nod
not
nun
nut

O
off
on

P
pan
pat
pay
peep
peg
pen
pet
pig
pill
pin
pip
pit
play
pop
pot
pull
pump
pup

R
rag
ram
ramp
ran
rat
ray
red
rib
rim
rob
rod
rub
rug
run
rub
rug
run

S
sad
sag
sap
sat
say
see
seed
seen
sell
set
she
shed
shell
shin
ship
shop
shot
shut
sip
sit
six
slab
slam
slap
sled
slim
slip
slit
slop
slot
slug
small
smell
smog
snag
snap
snip
snob
snug
sob
span
speed
spell
spill
spin
spit
spot
spy
stab
stall
stamp
star
stay
steep
stem
step
still
stop
stub
stun
sum
sun
swag
swan
sway
sweep
sweet
swell
swim

Your Spelling Words

T
tag
tall
tan
tap
tar
tell
ten
tin
tip
to
today
top
tray
tree
tub
tug

U
up

V
van
vet

W
wag
wall
wax
way
web
weed
week
weep
well
wet
wig
will
win

Y
yap
yell
yes
yet

Your Own Words

A

B

C

D

E

F

G

H

Your Own Words

I

J

K

L

M

N

O

P

Your Own Words

Q

R

S

T

U

V

W

X Y Z

Record of Progress

Unit	Date Completed	Teacher's Comments
1 The Alphabet		
2 b as in bag		
3 d as in dog		
4 t as in tap		
5 g as in gum		
6 p as in pet		
7 a (bat, ran)		
8 e (bed, pen)		
9 i (pin, lid)		
10 o (pot, box)		
11 u (bun, pup)		
Review 1		
12 c as in cat		
13 f as in fan		
14 h as in ham		
15 l as in log		
16 m as in man		
17 n as in nip		
18 ee as in feed		
Review 2		

Record of Progress

Unit	Date Completed	Teacher's Comments
19 r as in rat		
20 s as in sat		
21 vwy as in van wet yes		
22 j as in jug		
23 k as in kit		
24 all as in ball		
25 ell as in bell		
26 ill as in bill		
ull as in bull		
Review 3		
27 ch as in chop		
28 sh as in shed		
29 sl as in slap		
30 sm as in smog		
sn as in snap		
31 sp as in spin		
32 st as in stop		
33 sw as in swim		
34 mp as in lamp		
35 ar as in car		
36 ay as in day		
Review 4		